The Man In The White Coat

A Veterinarian's Tail of Love

By

Roger L. Welton, DVM

Dedicated to my heart and soul, Austin Lee and Scarlett Isabella

Prologue

It may seem odd to some that in my mid 40's I would choose to write memoirs about a career that did not even start until my mid-twenties given all of the years of school required to achieve a veterinary degree. To me, however, middle age is absolutely the appropriate time to publish memoirs, albeit having hardly crossed the halfway mark of my veterinary career, yet in the greater scheme, now living in the twilight of a journey that began at the age of 3. I will not give away the life changing event that marked that integral year of my life that made veterinary medicine my imminent path, but suffice it to say that although that year and the years that followed may not have been all filled with educational and clinical experience, they still were filled with experiences that were significant contributors to the man and the veterinarian I became.

While the veterinary educational experience and a veterinary career are extraordinary, they are ultimately the culmination and realization of love of and reverence for animals, uniquely coupled with a passion for science and the scientific method. These attributes do not suddenly appear out of thin air, but have their roots in who we are as people, what we experience in life, and the people that inspire us along the way.

Thus, when you ask most veterinarians at what point they knew that veterinary medicine was the career path for them; the vast majority will tell you that it started at a very young age. It is the likely explanation why a good number of my blog readers and podcast listeners are elementary school, middle school and high school students. Similarly, I would not be surprised if many who choose to read this book are young people as well who like I once was, are on the path that I started at 3; perhaps not even yet in college, but seeking some insight into the journey of the veterinarian.

To those of you reading my book simply to get a glimpse of what drives a person to become a veterinarian, what it is like to be a veterinarian, or to share in the good feelings that come with moving stories of pets and the people who love them, enjoy, and thank you for caring to read. To my readers who are on the path of a budding veterinarian, my advice to you is to not only enjoy these pages, but hopefully learn from them and to savor every moment of your own journey. The road to achieving our goals is not paved in gold but instead paved with ups and downs, triumph and failure, elation and grief. These collective states of mind and experiences are essential in forming the professionals, business owners, spouses, parents, and community people you will one day be.

Future doctors of veterinary medicine tend to be so driven and conscientious with their eye on the prize, that all too often, they find themselves one day well into their careers and look back regretting that they did not take the time to appreciate each step that brought them there. Within these pages, you will read tails (as I call them) of joy and sadness, success and failure, contentment and frustration; but underlying all of those peaks and valleys of experience, one sentiment permeated and transcended them all...love.

Chapter 1 –"Animals are such agreeable friends, they ask no questions, they pass no criticisms" - *George Eliot*

Truthfully, my memory of age of 3 is as foggy as anyone's. Like most people, I do not remember a cohesive narrative of my life experience back then, but instead just a combination of significant memory snippets that stand out, and anecdotes from my parents to fill in the blanks.

We had just moved to the township of Clark, NJ, the community that I would ultimately grow up in. My father worked a full time job by day and went to school at night on the GI Bill, while my Mom was at home with my brother and me. My 7 year old brother was in school full time, and still new to the town, my family had not had the opportunity yet to network and have ample outreach for play dates for their 3 year old boy. My Mom was tasked with maintaining the home, doing all of the shopping, making sure my brother was ready for school, having his homework done, and keep both of us fed and clothed. She did not have every moment available to spend entertaining me.

This certainly is no tale of woe, as I really enjoyed my alone time in the backyard. Although Clark was technically a suburb of New York City, it had a lot of trees, woods, and wildlife. In my backyard was an enormous oak tree with several other smaller ones that kept me entertained for hours as I watched the squirrels play and gather nuts, birds fly, nest and feed their young, and raccoons begin to congregate at dusk.

While this certainly began to pique my fascination with animals, it was also the beginning of a passion for how nature and the world around us worked. I used to dig until I reached earthworms and then watch them as they wriggled along and burrowed back into the ground. Caterpillars, inchworms, honey bees, and butterflies were all objects of my intense observations. Indeed the scientist in me had awakened at a very young age.

My back yard might as well have been Yellowstone National Park in my imagination, and I could not wait to get out there each day. From my recollection and what my parents had told me, despite the absence of my brother at school most of the day and having no real friends yet, I was a happy child, content to spend my days alone in my own little world of "nature." What I did not know was that I was not to be alone much longer.

My mother was originally born in Bogota, Colombia, and many of her immediate and extended family was still there. Naturally, we took periodic family trips there, and in one such trip around this time, my older cousin Patricia's English Cocker Spaniel, Archie, had just sired a litter of puppies. To our delight, my brother and I got to hold and play with the puppies during our visit, an amazing experience for young boys. Raised Catholic, my brother was to complete his First Holy Communion that year, and unbeknownst to us, one of those puppies was slated to be his gift for completing this milestone Catholic sacrament.

Sometime after we had returned home and my brother had completed his Communion, my Uncle Fernando arrived one evening with a 16 week old black English Cocker Spaniel puppy named Waldo. Uncle "Fernie," like my Mom, had immigrated to the US and had agreed to fly Waldo back with him on one of his visits back to Bogota. My brother and I were besides ourselves with joy, absolutely floored that one of those puppies we had so enjoyed on our trip to Colombia was now ours to keep!

While of course my parents refrained from telling me that Waldo was actually a gift for my brother, they secretly let him know, and that he would need to step up and take responsibility to house train, feed, clean up after, and let Waldo out. At first, my brother readily accepted his new responsibility. But guess who was even more readily eager to help?

Over time for my brother the novelty of Waldo began to wear off. Whereas he previously would feed him and put out fresh water for him with enthusiasm, it now was becoming a chore. By 4 years old, I concentrated to learn how to operate a can opener (there were no pop cans for canned goods in the late 1970s) to feed the dog and was able to pull up the stool to the sink so that I could refresh Waldo's water. My brother had no reservations in letting me take over Waldo's care.

Most importantly, in addition to reveling in my new responsibilities to care for the dog I now viewed as my dog (the fact that Waldo was originally a present to my brother was not revealed to me until I was an adult), I had a companion to spend every minute of every day with. Waldo also slept in my bed every night, and I just could not imagine life without him.

Although at a very young age Waldo had taught me the depth of the love and joy of the human-animal bond, I still knew nothing of the doctors charged with treating them when they were sick or injured. Two life changing incidents that occurred in fairly close succession that involved Waldo would change that lack of awareness, and forever mark my life's purpose.

Chapter 2 - "The best doctor in the world is the veterinarian, they can't ask their patients what is the matter, they've just got to know" - *Will Rogers*

Waldo was a delightfully playful and gentle creature, but like most young dogs, had a bit of a naughty side. One of his most naughty habits was to dump the garbage and feast on the delicacies within. My parents purchased all manner of different garbage contraptions to keep the dog from getting to the contents, but ultimately, Waldo was quite the Harry Houdini when it came to outsmarting the garbage bin.

Further compounding Waldo's keen interest in the kitchen trash bin, was the fact that he was regularly fed treats from the dinner table. Waldo was our first family dog and we could not resist his sad little Cocker Spaniel eyes conveying how passionately he craved just a little taste of what we were eating. The worst offender of all was Mom. Even when we were out to dinner, Mom would now allow our scraps to be taken away without first having the opportunity to fill the doggy bag for Waldo.

Thus, between a combination of a keen sense of taste for human food and an uncanny ability to circumvent any and all garbage securing lids, the ultimate method to keep the dog from the trash in the end was good garbage vigilance and timely changing out of particularly appealing trash that contained food scraps and bones.

By this time, my Mom was pregnant with my sister, I was well into preschool, my brother was in 4th grade, and my father was still about as busy as ever. As much as garbage patrol was a family priority, the occasional oversight occurred and, ever the opportunist, Waldo would take full advantage and treat us with a kitchen floor full of chewed up trash, shredded trash bags, and the pleasure of foul gas that often accompanied his "garbage can gut." We never actually heard Waldo's farts, but boy could he clear a room after his gut was particularly sour following a meal of garbage!

One night, the contents of the garbage were particularly appealing, while at the same time being particularly dangerous: chicken bones. Most dogs' jaws and teeth are capable of breaking chicken bones, with the subsequent splintered shards of bones posing a significant obstruction or gut laceration hazard. Even as novice dog owners, we were aware of this, which left my parents very concerned after they encountered the garbage full of chicken bones having been accessed and chewed up by Waldo with most of the bones missing.

Of course, Waldo seemed happy as a clam despite his dietary indiscretion, but that would precipitously change by the next day. It began with Waldo, still essentially an overgrown puppy, being depressed and lethargic. The most striking sign was Waldo refusing food...that was most definitely out of character, as this was a dog that never missed a meal. Once things progressed to him straining and crying as he tried to have a bowel movement with no success with only drops of blood coming out, my parents decided it was time to rush him to the vet.

I recall my Dad wanted me to stay home, but I insisted on going along. Waldo was my best friend and he was sick and in pain...my Dad would have had to handcuff me to my bed to keep me from going with Waldo to the vet. My Dad must have suspected that things may get unpleasant and wanted to spare me that. The whole family knew how emotional I was about my dog.

We were escorted into an exam room and shortly after in walked a man in a white coat who apparently was the person who was going to try to help my very sick dog. The man in the white coat was very friendly and patiently and courteously listened to the history my Dad provided him. He then very gently examined Waldo and talked reassuringly to him as he looked him over.

I remember the man in the white coat pressing on Waldo's tummy and Waldo letting out a cry and he told Waldo he was sorry and pet him gently to calm him down. Although I was upset to see Waldo yelp in pain, I felt at ease that this man truly cared about Waldo and sincerely wanted to help him.

I do not know exactly how the veterinarian determined that Waldo was obstructed with bones, but I recall him telling us that the chicken bones that were stuck had traveled far enough that he could probably be able to pull them out without the need for surgery. He gave Waldo an injection, which in hindsight must have been a sedative or pain reliever of some kind.

The veterinarian then put on a latex glove, lifted Waldo's tail, and proceeded to manually pull out several shards of bone. Between Waldo crying through the procedure and seeing the blood on the gloves of the vet, I was naturally very upset about the ordeal. Through it all, though, I did not cry, and I did not blame the vet for what he was doing to my dog. I recall that he seemed like a very kind man, and I trusted that he aimed only to help Waldo; and help him he did.

Waldo was released shortly thereafter, regained his appetite, and was able to have bowel movements again, and sent home on pills – again in hindsight, likely antibiotics. My very sick dog was well again, all because of the kind man in the white coat. From that day forth, I knew what I wanted to do with my life.

Most people cannot state that they discovered their calling in life at the age of 4, but for me, it could not have been clearer that I wanted to be that kind man in the white coat, able to heal a little boy's best friend. Less than one year later, I would see the man in the white coat heal my dog yet again.

I do not recall who exactly it was that was cooking in the kitchen, but I remember the fire like it was yesterday. An oil fire broke out in a cooking pan on the range top. The fire was as sudden as it was intense, and my Dad grabbed oven gloves to bring the pan over to the sink, but in transit, some of the oil splashed on to the dining room carpet adjacent to the kitchen linoleum and instantly ignited it. Both my parents at that point yelled for us to get out of the house, which we quickly did. My brother ran to the neighbor's house yelling "fire," and there was so much commotion, that I did not realize Waldo was still in the house until I saw him run out on his own, with his rear end smoking, crying in agony, as he rolled all over the front lawn. My neighbor at this point was inside having grabbed a fire extinguisher and dousing out the fire, but I was not concerned with what was going on in the house; all I could see was that my dog was hurt and in pain.

The fire now put out and the damage having been contained to the kitchen and dining room, all attention was now on Waldo, who had suffered a large burn over his back, just in front of the base of his tail, about the size and shape of a potato. The hair had been scorched off and skin beneath blistered and blackened. I do not recall how much time elapsed or exactly when we found ourselves once again at the vet, but I do remember Waldo receiving treatment from that kind man in the white coat once again. He told us that aside from a scar where hair would not likely regrow that everything would be fine and he gave us pills to give Waldo, as well as an ointment to apply to the wound.

Exactly as the vet he said, Waldo did make a full recovery, but he kept that scar for the rest of his life, a long lasting physical reminder of how lucky we were that, while it was unfortunate that poor Waldo had gotten hurt, we as a family had been spared a much greater tragedy. For me, it was also a constant reminder of what I wanted to be when I grew up: the man in the white coat.

Chapter 3- Duck love is recognizable in any language" - *Edmond Manning*

It goes without saying that Waldo was a huge part of my life, leading some of my neighbors to jokingly compare me to Dennis the Menace and his dog. I am pretty sure that this comparison went beyond my relationship with my dog and they found me a bit of a nuisance as well. At any rate, Waldo was my constant companion and play mate, truly my first best friend. I had human friends, of course, and when I played with them, Waldo was always part of the fun. Some of my friends found my love of my dog a little weird, but my best friends – guys that I am still tight with to this day – understood that love of Waldo and animals, was a significant part of who and what I was...they still understand it to this day.

Whether I was rescuing a turtle slowly crossing the street at risk of getting hit by a car,, saving a terrified kitten from a tree, or just sitting on the grass in my backyard delighted to watch the squirrels chase each other and play in our huge oak tree; animals were always my primary source of fascination and love. Something about them just spoke to me.

During a particularly humorous spring/summer, my family and I had been vacationing in Miami as we often did every spring break to see our extended family down there. I was about 12 years old and my Aunt Carmen, affectionately known by all of her nieces and nephews as "Chachi," had moved into a brand new, quaint condominium complex in West Miami. One of the best aspects of her complex – at least from my perspective – was all of the beautiful retention lakes with fountains, with countless beautiful white ducks everywhere.

The ducks were very accustomed to people with many of the residents enjoying strolling about the trails that tracked around the lakes and feeding them all of the time, so they usually would not hesitate to get a within a few feet of us. Since we often visited my family in Miami during spring break, a time when many animal species reproduce, I got to witness the absolute beauty of families of ducks with their ducklings. My love of ducks stays with me to this day.

Anyway, my fascination and love of the ducks led me one night to do something very irresponsible. There was a duck near my aunt's condominium that was a female sitting on her eggs. When she got up to go take a swim, I ran over and grabbed an egg. My plan was to incubate and hatch the egg and raise a little duckling of my own. My parents were not happy with what I did, but by the time they found out, they figured that at that point that they might as well let me do my thing and who knows, maybe the egg would hatch. Their decision was also influenced by the old wives tale pervasive at the time, that once a bird smelled human on its offspring, it would reject it, so replacing it was out of the question.

The rest of the vacation, I never went anywhere without my duck egg, playing momma duck and keeping it in my hands to keep the egg warm. I even took it to the beach, where I would wrap it in soft towels under the shade of our beach umbrella so that it would not overheat while I was in the water. We had driven down to Miami, so I did not have to try to explain boarding a plane with an egg cradled in my hands, and I held and warmed the egg the whole ride back. My brother, 16 at the time, thought I was crazy.

Back in NJ, the egg never hatched. Eventually, I cracked the egg open to find red slime inside, not fetal structures of any kind. I really did not understand then, but as the result of my handling of the egg and removing it from mom, my guess in hindsight, is that my intervention likely halted the development of an embryo.

Not understanding exactly why but having a sense that I was likely the cause of a duckling that would never be, I felt awful. My Aunt Chachi felt bad for me knowing what I was experiencing, and was moved by how much I loved the ducks in her complex. Chachi was never one to resist the temptation to indulge the whims of her beloved nieces and nephews. She never had children of her own, so she treated us like we were her own.

She decided as an early birthday present, to purchase two ducklings and have them FedEx'd from Miami to our home in NJ. Thus, I came home from school one day to find two beautiful ducklings in my house, so small that each fit in the palms of my hands. Chachi sent two so that I could claim one and my sister could claim one so that there would be no fighting over the ducklings. My brother by this time was 16 years old and his interest in girls and his social life far outweighed any interest he would have in ducks.

Chachi had not cleared this with my parents who likely would have disagreed with this gift. Pet ducks in suburban NJ only 8 miles from New York City was not only impractical, but outright strange. Of course, there was no sending them back after my sister and I got our hands on them, so my parents begrudgingly accepted this one.

I picked the duckling with brown feet with a brown beak, because these were unusual traits for this particular breed of duck. Most had orange feet with orange beaks. I named my duck Clarence. My sister named her duck Martha, after my Mom. This was pretty ironic, since my Mom held a deep seeded childhood phobia of birds as the result of having been terrified watching Alfred Hitchcock's The Birds. (Please read on, because the story of Martha and my Mom eventually gets down right hilarious!)

So the ducklings were adorable and even my Mom and Dad had to admit how much fun they were paddling around in the baby pool we got them and having imprinted on us, waddling around the yard following after us. My parents found it particularly amusing when they would come home and I would be lying down in the front lawn gazing up at the sky with Clarence curled up, asleep on my chest.

Clarence grew up to be stunning. He kept the brown feet and beak, but he was solid white and sweet as can be. Martha, on the other hand, grew this red, proud fleshy tissue around her eyes and had black streaks....she kind of took on this look of being a duck/turkey hybrid. While both ducks grew to be large, Martha was huge, nearly two times the size of Clarence; bigger than most Thanksgiving turkeys I have ever seen. In addition, she was not quite as sweet as Clarence, a bit more independent and stand-offish, and then eventually she would become outright ornery. And so began the gradual end of the duck honeymoon.

The first problem was that despite us having upgraded the size and scope of their baby pool, they far preferred our actual swimming pool to swim in. My Dad in particular had a great deal of pride in our family swimming pool, and the ducks indiscriminately defecating in the pool did not sit well with him.

As ducks would naturally do, they learned to fly and it was eventually not uncommon to come home to find them perched on a neighbor's roof resting – and defecating – on their roofs. The neighbors were not happy and it was likely that we were in violation of a few town ordinances having livestock living in our yard.

The last straw, however, came when Martha's demeanor became downright nasty and she would spread her wings, jump up and down, then attack and peck at people's ankles and feet as they entered the yard. My Mom became a prisoner in her own home, unwilling to go in her own back yard for fear of the dreaded Martha the duck that ironically bore her namesake.

One night, my Mom had a tray of marinated steaks she was determined to grill in the backyard. Martha and Clarence were sleeping, so she deftly and quietly moseyed over to the grill with the tray of raw meat. Martha must have heard her and did what Martha usually did as someone entered the yard. From inside the house, I heard my Mom screaming as she ran in the back door almost in tears. In her panic, my Mom had left a rather expensive tray of raw meat in the middle of the yard so as to hasten her escape from Martha the duck; which I thankfully ran out to rescue in time so at least family dinner was not ruined.

My parents knew how much I loved Clarence, so they knew they would have to remove the ducks on the sly knowing the argument I would put forth. Thus, one day I came home to find my yard devoid of ducks and it hit home when I saw that their great big duck pen that my Dad had had built for them was gone. My Mom broke the news to me that we simply could no longer keep the ducks, but they would be happy living out the rest of their lives on a farm in West NJ.

I was crushed, but as much as I knew I would miss them, I also knew and accepted that the decision my parents made was for the best. Luckily, I was able to shake that off in good time, as I would soon have to confront a far more grievous loss.

Chapter -4 "I guess you don't really own a dog, you rent them, and you have to be grateful that you had a long lease." - *Joe Garagiola*

Waldo was aging gracefully at 11 years of age. Sure he slept a bit more but he could still run around the backyard and neighborhood with me and on the plus side, he was no longer humping everything that moved every spring (my Dad would not allow Waldo neutered as he deemed it inhumane as many men of that time did). By this time, I was in middle school and had a lot of human friends and other interests, namely lacrosse and girls.

I hung out with my friends at Friday night rec, a town youth club where kids could safely play sports and safely – and mostly appropriately – socially gather with adult chaperones about. It was something that that my home town of Clark, NJ really got right. I also went to the movies, raced BMX bikes in the woods, and played manhunt.

I still always found time for Waldo, my original friend whether it was spending time with him in the backyard, taking him for walks, snuggling on the couch and watching Rambo for the 10th time, and of course, sleeping in my bed every night.

One day, Waldo started getting weird skin rashes. They made him itch like crazy and he frequently lost patches of hair. His veterinarian at first did not quite know what to make of it until one day we brought Waldo in with a 2 cm skin mass over his back that suddenly appeared seemingly overnight. Dr. Tucker, his kind veterinarian for many years, recommended removing the mass and having it sent off to be analyzed, which my parents did not hesitate to schedule.

I don't recall how many days had elapsed since the surgery, but I do know that Waldo had completely healed by then (veterinary pathology must have taken longer back then) when my Mom came down to the basement in tears to talk to me. I remember like it was yesterday, lifting weights just as she entered the room. I stopped my biceps curls and asked her what was wrong. Mom gave me a bug and informed me that Waldo had cancer and he would not live much longer.

The odd thing was, although my Mom expected me to be devastated, I wasn't. I had very fortunately never really experienced serious loss at that point in my life. I knew of this dreaded cancer word only in theory – I knew it was bad and that it killed, but the gravity just did not hit me. From what I could see, the ugly tumor was gone and Waldo only had some skin rashes. Other than that, he was fine.

Only Waldo was not fine. His skin rashes got so bad and frequent; my Mom had to constantly bathe him and my parents would no longer allow him to sleep in bed with me, as they were concerned that he may get secondary infections that would put me at risk. My Mom prepared a bed for him, but Waldo was not interested. He had slept in bed snuggled with a human all of his life. A dog bed simply would not suffice and he would scratch at my door to be let in which would not only wake me up (I have always had trouble sleeping), but I would always let him in. How could I not?

Eventually, Waldo's dog bed got moved to the basement. While our basement was a finished basement with couches, carpeting, a big TV, a full service bar, a laundry room and a home gym, but it was still a place my best friend had to sleep by himself. Many nights, I laid a towel down next to his dog bed and would fall asleep next to him. It was so hard to say goodnight to him and leave there.

One evening, we went out to a steakhouse and, true to form, we came home with a doggy bag for Waldo full of prime rib leftovers. Despite living with cancer, he was still just as excited as ever to receive his treat. As we fed it to him, we watched heartbroken as our boy who would normally devour such a treat in a few seconds flat, instead struggled to swallow his food. He had to keep spitting out the steak and re-chewing time and again to get it down. What used to take seconds took nearly 10 minutes. I tried massaging his throat to help him swallow and I remember feeling big lumps in his neck. In hindsight, now a practicing veterinarian, I know that what I felt were severely enlarged lymph nodes. Whatever cancer had started in his skin had spread to his lymph nodes and the rest of his body.

A short time later, I do not remember exactly how long, I came home from school and Waldo was not there. My Dad had taken him to the vet to have him humanely euthanized. My parents did not tell me so as to not have me agonize over the decision and instead help me grieve his loss. My Mom, amazingly composed, broke the news to me.

Oddly, while I felt the shock and the loss, rather than suffer from intense grief, in a strange way I felt relief. The relief was not just for the end of my dog's suffering, but for an end of my own suffering as I watched my best friend weaken over several months. I did not cry at that moment. I did not suppress it; the flood of grief just never came.

But one night, I am not sure if it was weeks or even months later, I was lying in bed unable to sleep which was not unusual, watching a Star Trek rerun, which was also not unusual. I remembered so many other sleepless nights that I watched Star Trek reruns (and often Twilight Zone reruns after that, I was such as bad insomniac) that I took comfort in feeling my warm, snoring dog snuggled next to me.

At that moment, the shock had worn off, the relief was gone, and all that was left was loss, and the pain seemed at that moment more than I could bear. I never told anyone and as I write these words as a grown middle aged man, it is hard to suppress those tears from returning. I felt as though Waldo was irreplaceable, that I could never love a dog the way I loved Waldo, and that any dog (or any pet for that matter) would be done an injustice because I would always know that he was not my beloved Waldo.

Chapter – 5 "Life is a series of Dogs" – *George Carlin*

One of my favorite comedians, George Carlin, one said that life is a series of dogs, as every era of the life of a dog lover can be ascribed to the particular dog or dogs one may have had during that time. While Waldo was the dog of my boyhood, the dog for the next era of my life would also be another English Cocker Spaniel, one who not only looked quite differently from Waldo, but had an entirely different personality and relationship with me altogether.

As we had all grieved the loss of Waldo, the entire Welton family felt the void of no longer having a furry little family member to love. With my 14th birthday coming up, my Mom had been researching English Cocker Spaniel breeders in our area and found one in Brick, NJ that had just had a litter of light buff colored, show quality, English Cocker Spaniels.

We took a family trip down to Brick to see the 8 week old puppies and instantly fell in love with all of them. I still had the nagging feeling that there was not enough room in my heart to love another dog as I did Waldo, but watching 8 week old puppies gleefully frolicking around the yard was enough to help soothe any broken heart. My Dad settled on a particularly rambunctious puppy among the litter thinking that it was best to pick the most active and playful of the bunch, but we would have to wait another 4 weeks to bring him home. This was a reputable and ethical breeder who understood that a litter should stay together with Mom until 12 weeks of age for physical and mental health reasons.

Being the right thing to do as it was, waiting 4 weeks to pick up our puppy was agonizing for my sister and me! It was all we could think about day and night for a month! But alas, one thing we can always count on is that time always marches on and our puppy inevitably arrived.

Our reunion with the puppy we would name Stanley was a glorious love fest at first. We could not do much else but play with him and stare at him as he romped around the house and the backyard. He was beautiful inside and out, light buff in color with huge, expressive dark brown eyes and as playful and sweet as any puppy could be.

Oh, but he had a dark side. The Welton family had grown long accustomed to life with our senior aged Waldo. We had long forgotten how naughty and mischievous – and destructive – puppies could be! Waldo's puppy naughtiness paled in comparison to Stanley's.

Not one hour would seemingly go by without finding a slipper chewed, a pillow torn open, or even carpet ripped up. I recall one time he chewed up a very expensive pair of my Dad's work loafers (my father had to wear a suit to work every day and his wardrobe was very important to him). He was none too happy to see an expensive pair of shoes treated like pieces of rawhide.

Another time, he somehow tipped over my Mom's make up box from her vanity, chewed up all her make up pads, brushes and lipstick, meanwhile covering himself head to toe in multi-colored make-up. My childhood best friend Steve (who remains so to this day) nicknamed Stanley, "Destruction."

Nonetheless, as frustrating as Destruction could be as we encountered him destroying some of our most important or cherished household and personal items, we loved him dearly. This was the first time I was to learn that a new pet is not a replacement for a lost pet, but a whole new experience with a whole different kind of love for a whole new set of reasons. The lost pet remains instilled in your heart for all time, while the new one just occupies his/her own area of your heart.

I ultimately loved Stanley no less than I did Waldo, just differently. Not only was Stanley nothing like Waldo, he accompanied me on my life's journey that was a completely different era of my life than the one Waldo travelled with me. True to George Carlin's famous quote, while Waldo was with me during the innocent and formative years of my childhood, Stanley would be the dog that represented my teenage years and all of the changes that came during that time as I transitioned from boy to young man.

Chapter – 6 "Changes Come Around Real Soon Make Us Women And Men" – *John Mellencamp*

Stanley's arrival coincided with a very exciting – and very confusing – time of a typical boy's life. I was about a month from turning 14 and within weeks of graduating from 8th grade and high school was around the corner. At this time, I was very active in sports, my favorite of which was lacrosse, had an active and fun social life, and had a keen interest especially in girls. School, socializing, and extracurricular activities took up a significant amount of my time.

That is not to say I did not engage with my dog, Stanley, he just did not have the same central role in my life that Waldo played in my boyhood. Despite having so many other facets of my life, I still walked him constantly, trained him, fed him, swam with him, and of course he slept in my bed every night. He laid at my feet as I did my homework and laid next to me on the couch when I watch MTV (back when they actually played music on MTV). I also soon learned that Stanley was a chick magnet, so I often took advantage of the opportunity to bring him along when a group of friends were gathering at a public park.

It was during this time that I first realized that not everyone cared for animals. While a lot of my peers really enjoyed Stanley, others were either indifferent or were even annoyed by him. I found this very strange. How could it even be possible that someone would not like being around a cute, playful dog? With Stanley and animals in general being such an important part of my life, I started to become weary of people that do not care for them. That is something that has not only stayed with me, but has become ever more prevalent in my view of people as time has gone on.

I recall I had a big crush on a girl named Melanie in the summer heading into 9th grade. She had invited me and a friend of mine over her house to hang out. Her parents would not allow boys in the house, so we would hang out in her front yard, which was a great opportunity to bring Stanley over as well.

As we arrived, Melanie did not pay any attention to the puppy and when he put his front legs on her for attention, she looked at me with an unpleasant expression on her face and said, "Get him off."

Needless to say, I was very turned off by this. As pretty as Melanie was, this shaved off several layers of attractiveness in my eyes and I had little interest in even staying another minute. Not surprisingly, I never ended up actually dating Melanie. In fact, we really were not even friends after then, I not only lost interest in her romantically, I really just had little interest in knowing her at all.

At the age of 16 during the summer of 1991 heading into my senior year, I was at Manasquan Inlet Beach at the Jersey Shore with my friends (our go to shore spot). There was a group of three beautiful girls sitting about 50 yards away from us the whole day. They would catch us glancing at them and we would catch them taking glances at us, but in 4 hours, none of us had the courage to walk over and say something. As we were leaving, we noticed that they were leaving as well and got into their car just in front of our parking spot and we pulled out right behind them. We were following them for 15 minutes (we were not stalking them; there was only one main road that led to the Garden State Parkway to head back up north). We were all thirsty and decided we were going to stop at a 7-11 for some drinks that we always passed on the way home from the beach, when what would you know, these same girls decided to pull in right then as well.

At this point, my friend Danny thought that this was way too much coincidence, that fate was telling us that we needed to meet these girls, so he popped out and struck up a conversation with them. Two of them were from the shore area, but one of them named Kristen, the one driving the car, was from a town neighboring our hometown of Clark, NJ. We all chatted for a bit and Kristen gave Danny her number for us to give her a call the next time we were planning on heading down to the shore (Clark was about a 45 minute drive north of Manasquan). One of the other local shore girls in the car was Kristen's cousin, the one I was originally interested in (Kristen was beautiful and seemed nice, but it seemed she and my friend Danny had hit it off).

Upon returning back to Clark, Danny handed me Kristen's number and suggested I call her since he had a girlfriend in Clark and was feeling guilty about taking the number. I thought it might seem very strange for me to call, having barely said three words to Kristen, and was not the guy she gave her number to. I held onto her number for a few days nonetheless when finally I decided that I had nothing to lose and picked up the phone and called her.

I explained to Kristen that I was one of the guys she met at the shore, but not the one she gave her number to. I let her know that he had a girlfriend and felt guilty, so he instead gave me her number to call and conveniently enough, I was single. Amazingly, she remembered instantly which of the Clark boys I was and did not find it weird at all that I called! We talked for over an hour and learned that we were barely one degree of separation from one another, as I went to school with and knew her step brother who actually lived with his Mom in Clark.

Before getting off the phone, I asked her if she wanted to go out the upcoming weekend, to which she enthusiastically said yes. I was a bit embarrassed to have to ask her to pick me up, as I was not yet old enough to drive. She just good naturedly chuckled and said that would be fine.

I will not go through the play by play of that summer's courting ritual between Kristen and me, but we really hit it off. She was not only beautiful (5'8, thin but curvy frame, black hair with big, brown, expressive eyes that reminded me of the actress Phoebe Kates) but she was smart, funny, fun to be around, and my friends all loved her as well. My dog Stanley was also quite smitten with her and she returned all of the affection he showed her, never missing an opportunity to scratch his tummy and play with him.

I know most people understand what it was like to experience one's first love. It was an indescribable feeling to be with someone that I was not only incredibly attracted to, but someone I could be myself around, someone I trusted implicitly, walking around feeling as if I was on a cloud and my soul had merged with another's. As we entered our senior years at our respective high schools, our relationship continued to grow and thrive. While we enjoyed the group social life, we were increasingly content to spend time with just one another; instead of spending weekend evenings out with our friends, we often instead opted to go to Blockbuster Video to rent a movie (my millennial readers will have no idea what this is - just Google it), and snuggle on the couch watching it with Stanley between us.

Kristen's high school did not have a lacrosse team, so in the spring, she would bring her friends along to my games to watch and she wore my varsity lacrosse jacket at her school (which I thought was awesome). In the NJ State Championship tournament, we drew Mountain Lakes, a town in West Jersey about a 40 minute drive west of where we lived. Kristen drove out to my game, as we progressed to through the post-season, each game became increasingly tough and important. Mountain Lakes was a team we had not faced during the season, but they matched up against us well and we knew we were in for a battle.

Roger Welton, Spring 1992

This game was not only a tough matchup of talent, but it was a very physical game from the opening face-off. Both teams traded goals and big hits and it was anyone's game. In the third quarter, I took a lefty shot in traffic and with my left shoulder exposed, and then took a big hit from a much larger Mountain Lakes defensemen and I heard a loud crack. I knew instantly that I had broken my collarbone.

As the paramedics carried me off on a stretcher, I had tears, but not from the pain. Although the injury did indeed hurt, my tears came from leaving my team and my best friends in the midst of the most important game we had ever played in our past 7 years together. I was heartbroken that win or lose, this was the last high school lacrosse game I would ever play. By this time I had already committed to Montclair State University to play college lacrosse, but that was the furthest thing from my mind.

Kristen and my brother were with me from the field to the hospital where my fracture was treated. As much as I loved my older brother and appreciated his support of my lacrosse career, the most reassuring presence I had was Kristen. She knew me so well, understood the depth of my love of lacrosse, my team, and my friends who I had battled alongside since 6th grade. I saw the empathy in her eyes and I could not have imagined a more comforting presence at that moment.

The attending doctor gave me a potent injection of some kind of opioid for the pain that made me quite loopy and sleepy. When my parents came to pick me up, Kristen followed us home. I was in and out of sleep most of the evening, but she stayed right by my side until she had to leave to not break her curfew.

That spring, we went to one another's proms. My prom was before the Mountain Lakes game, so I was not injured for mine. Unfortunately, her prom was after the Mountain Lakes game, so I had to attend it in with my arm in a sling and a fresh fracture. For those who have never broken their collar bone, it is really uncomfortable. Being the only bone structure that attaches the arm to the trunk, any movements, even coughing or laughing, could send a sharp pain to the shoulder and make you see stars.

Needless to say, I was a pretty lame date at Kristen's prom, but she cheerfully made the best of it and so did I. We also attended one another's graduation ceremonies.

Although Kristen and I had a fun summer to look forward to, we both knew that imminent separation from one another loomed with both of us slated to start college at the end of the summer. I was to attend Montclair State as I stated earlier in late August, she was to start school at West Chester University in Pennsylvania in early September. The schools were about a 2 ½ hour drive from one another depending on NJ Turnpike traffic, but at that age, it felt like it may as well be on the other side of the country. Compounding this pending doom, we both knew my playing schedule would consume a lot of my time and inhibit our ability to drive to see each other. Still, we determined to have a great last summer together and fully intended to make our relationship work.

Every summer, the Welton family vacation was usually in Florida where we had family on both sides and both of my grandmothers lived: My Mom's mother, who we called Abuelita, lived in Miami, and my Dad's mother who we called Grandma, lived in Tampa. Thus we would usually drive so that we could easily split our time in both areas of Florida over 2 weeks without renting a car and it allowed us to bring Stanley along. In the summer of 1992, my Mom suggested Kristen come along, and we were both ecstatic when her Mom agreed to it. We were both 18 by this time, but we still had to sleep in separate bedrooms for most of the vacation.

We spent the first week of vacation with the whole family in Miami with my Abuelita and my Colombian relatives on my Mom's side of the family. We enjoyed South Beach with its beautiful beaches, great shopping and great food and nightlife, but a few nights, we just had dinner with the family, went out for ice cream, and took Stanley for evening walks.

On week two, we broke off from the Welton clan to travel to see my Grandma in Tampa, ideal for me to show Kristen the other coast of Florida, meet my Grandma, and Tampa is only an hour drive from Disney, which was on our itinerary. One of the nice things about seeing Grandma was that she was not all that politically correct. She drove a Camaro Z28, was known to drop the occasional swear word, and upon arrival, showed us to the master bedroom of her condo where we would be sleeping in the same room! Oh yes, my Grandma was very cool!

Of course, we also brought Stanley with us. My Grandma was quite the animal lover as well and was happy to have him. The Magic Kingdom had an air conditioned, deluxe kennel with spacious runs, and the guests were walked several times throughout the day. Stanley even got a Mickey Mouse certificate of exemplary canine behavior after his one day stay at the kennel.

We had a wonderful day at Disney, the picture perfect young couple basking in our love for one another, constantly holding hands, smiling and enjoying the rides and innocence of the Disney experience. We both felt like we were living in a dream, one we never wanted to wake from, blocking out our pending separation only a few weeks away, and living in the moment.

After Disney, we spent the rest of our days and evenings with my Grandma and my Uncle Billy (my Dad's brother), lounged at the pool of my Grandma's high rise condo by day, and walked Stanley around its beautiful grounds by night.

I was smitten and content. I could not picture ever feeling this way about anyone else. I most certainly could not imagine how I was going to remotely enjoy college without her there with me, nor could she.

Nonetheless, college loomed as the goal I had been working toward throughout high school. I was about to fulfill my goal, to major in biochemistry at a high academic achievement university as the first big step toward my veterinary career, while playing college lacrosse. I was so conflicted in how I felt on one hand about to experience the realization of my academics and athletics goals, while pained at the thought of being separated from Kristen.

Like it or not, time waits for no man and the day I was to move into my dorm arrived.

Chapter 7 - "Collegiate life presents a student with innumerable opportunities..." - Kilroy J Oldster

The first day that students report to college is an exciting, emotional, and chaotic time. Kristen was still a full week from when she had to report to Westchester, so she came with my parents to get me moved in. There were students, parents, suitcases, guitars, fish tanks, and any other manner of paraphernalia students brought with them to college.

I got placed in the only male only dorm on campus called Stone Hall. My high school buddy and lacrosse teammate Rich coincidentally also got placed in Stone Hall as well. He would be attending Montclair State with me as well, as both of us got recruited to play lacrosse for the Red Hawks. As we met other students, we quickly began to notice that there were a lot of other student athletes in Stone Hall. Rich's roommate was on the baseball team and my roommate was on the basketball team. Across the hall from me were twin brothers that were on the football team. It seemed that there was a plan to place at least freshman athletes in an all-male dorm perhaps to keep us less...distracted?

Kristen and my Mom helped me get moved in and settled that first day. My Mom left with tears in her eyes despite the fact that my campus was literally a 30 minute drive from home. I understand that the tears were more for her son taking a big next step to being less dependent on Mom and Dad. Kristen stayed over with me that first night.

That evening as we lay on my very uncomfortable dorm bed, it really hit us hard that for the first time in over a year, we would be apart for long periods of time. Of course we would call one another (there was no Facebook, Facetime, Skype, or even much email back then), but as everyone knows, when it comes to a loved one, telephone is a poor replacement for being physically present for one another.

There were lots of tears that evening and in the morning when Kristen had to leave. The day had a number of student orientation events that she could not attend. I would be starting classes for my biochemistry curriculum in only 2 days so we said our goodbyes knowing we would not see one another again until Thanksgiving break.

My roommate Mike struck me as a bit of an odd guy. He did not smile much and was generally grumpy but one of his first orders of business was to go out with his Dad's credit card and purchase a dorm refrigerator that he promptly filled with beer. Needless to say, we got acquainted rather quickly and I learned that Mike truly was grumpy, but hilarious and actually really fun to hang out with. I introduced him to Rich and we also befriended the football player twins across the hall and those guys would be my main core of friends throughout my time in college.

On a positive note, between making new friends, getting accustomed to college life, adjusting to a biochemistry field of study and many late night epic ping pong games in the common area with my new friends, I had little time to dwell on Kristen. I still missed her dearly and we spoke just about every other night, but the sting of separation eased over time. She also had made friends at West Chester and was going through her own adjustment to occupy her thoughts.

I did not meet my new lacrosse team for a few weeks, as lacrosse season is in the spring. In the fall, we generally just had periodic workouts and scrimmages. At our first team meeting, I felt pretty intimidated. With players ranging from 18 - 23 years of age, I felt like a boy surrounded by men that were bigger than me and had much thicker facial hair.   There was also the pecking order in team sports where the upperclassmen were not very friendly to freshman. I am thankful that there was no outright hazing, but they weren't really nice either. Case in point, although the # 20 that I had worn my entire high school playing career was available, my team captain would not allow me to have the number I wanted as a matter of principle that a freshman should not be issued the number he wants.

At any rate, the best way to endear yourself to your new team, freshman notwithstanding is to show you can play, and play I did. I would ultimately earn a starting spot as a freshman in the spring season of 1993 and go on to have a solid lacrosse career earning All-Conference honors twice. The team also cracked the top 20 in two of my four seasons with winning records in every season throughout my lacrosse career at Montclair State, as well as winning our conference all but one season.

My academic career started off very strong as well. Just glancing at my curriculum as I was registering for classes, seeing what seemed to be a daunting road ahead as a biochemistry major, I buckled down right out of the gate with regard to school. Through Thanksgiving break I enjoyed near perfect marks and was seemingly on my way to have the academic success I needed to get into veterinary school.

Chapter 8 - "Home is the place where, when you have to go there, they have to take you in." - *Robert Frost*

Thanksgiving break arrived before I knew it. Anyone who has ever gone away to college knows how fun Thanksgiving break is, getting to go back and see your family again, seeing all of your high school friends, and of course, reuniting with our significant others.

Seeing Kristen took my breath away. Like I previously stated, telephone was hardly a substitution for physical embrace, holding hands, or even just taking in the scent of her perfume. Whether we were partying with my high school buds, snuggling to watch a movie, or spending time with our families, we were inseparable and picked up right where we left off.

But my other reunion was a little family member I had not thought of much, to the extent that it made me feel guilty: my Cocker Spaniel Stanley! I realized it the moment I walked through the door, as Stanley was there to give me the most loving greeting he ever had. He was actually crying with joy as he jumped all over me. In turn, I was just as happy to see him and spent 10 minutes rolling around the floor with him and scratching his tummy.

It occurred to me instantly that in the years leading up to college, I had been Stanley's best friend. He slept in bed with me every night and followed me everywhere I walked in the house, snuggled on the couch with me when I watched TV, and I brought him along on car rides with me as often as I could.

My parents informed me that for the first week I was away at school, Stanley would walk upstairs to my room to see if I was there, and then walk back down after he did not see me. Rather than sleep in my room, he slept in a dog bed in my parent's room. However, once I was back home, he went right back to sleeping in bed with me. The love and loyalty of a dog is boundless.

Realizing how much I missed my dog and feeling guilty about not having given Stanley much thought in my first few months away from home, I spent as much time with Stanley as I could during that first homecoming. There was not yet any snow on the ground, so Kristen and I enjoyed a lot of park time with Stanley.

In the end, while it was wonderful to see so many that I loved during that first Thanksgiving break, it was only 4 days and they came and went in a flash. I returned to get right back into the rhythm of school, both socially and academically.

Chapter 9 - "To seek perfection is to find fault in the perfectly adequate, enjoyable, or even just plain good." - Ray Bennett, The Underachiever's Manifesto

Biochemistry at first presented itself as a daunting major as I first confronted my first semester courses: Calculus 1, Chemistry 1, Cell and Molecular Biology, and Physics 1 (there were other courses but they were either elective or base required curriculum like English Composition). As such, I took it very seriously in the first several weeks and my diligence paid off with very good grades as a result. However, I quickly learned that, like elementary and high school leading up to college, college academics, even biochemistry, came easy for me.

While this may seem to most people to be a blessing, to me it was also in a weird way, a curse, as it put me back into the mindset of academic complacency that pervaded my entire academic life. Despite having high standardized test scores, I was always a slightly better than average student in high school to the extent that without lacrosse, I would not have gotten accepted to Montclair State. It had nothing to do with ability and all to do with effort and priority. It is amazing how easy it was for me to so easily fall back into old patterns when I no longer feared the curriculum.

I cannot even begin to tell you how many times in my life my parents, teachers, and even peers told me that there is no reason that I should not be a straight A student. They were right. While I heard them, I never really listened to them, refusing to see the consequences that academic malaise would lead to; that the clock on fulfilling my dream to get accepted to veterinary school had begun to tick. In my mind, I would do well if not great, and really pick it up when it really mattered in later semesters as I got closer to submitting veterinary school applications.

Despite not putting in my best effort, my grades were most certainly not tanking, as I managed a 3.3 average throughout my undergraduate career. That would be considered by many of my biochemistry peers to be a respectable GPA. For veterinary school, however, that simply would not cut it, and by the time I fully realized it, it would be too late.

My big wakeup call came in my junior year when I took a part time job at a veterinary hospital near my school, Nutley Animal Hospital in Nutley, NJ. I had the good sense enough to know by then that veterinary schools favored students with hands on experience working in veterinary hospitals, clinics, and volunteering at shelters. The owner, Dr. Patrice McMahon, was willing to offer me a part time job that needed to work around my school schedule, while also working around the fact that I could not have a job in the spring during lacrosse season.

While working there, I met a young man named Adam who was a senior who had just gone through the veterinary school application process. He was set to attend Cornell University, College of Veterinary Medicine in the upcoming year, but he had just barely made it.

Adam had a stellar academic and work experience background having maintained a 3.9 GPA and worked part time for years at Nutley Animal Hospital, while volunteering to work at shelters and as a stable hand whenever he could throughout his undergraduate career. Despite his impressive record, Adam was waitlisted at Cornell, which was the only one of several schools he applied to that even granted him an interview.

I learned from Adam that since New Jersey had no state veterinary college, that state of NJ had contracts with 8 of the 27 U.S. veterinary schools, Cornell among them. Each school allotted NJ applicants 4 seats per school, meaning that there were a total of 32 spots per year awarded to thousands of applicants from the state of NJ. The competition for those spots was off the charts, and Adam got in only because a slot had opened up from a student who had been accepted that had turned down the spot for unknown reasons.

It dawned on me that if Adam with a near perfect record barely squeaked into veterinary school, what chance would I have with my 3.3? Granted, biochemistry was a more challenging major than most pre-veterinary students took on, but that would still not be enough to make up the difference of GPA that many applicants would have.

At this point just starting my junior year, I could have just kicked myself for not having taken the academic side more seriously. While I had a blast playing lacrosse and screwing around with my friends, those pursuits would soon lose their luster and I would realize that in having prioritized those pursuits more than I should have, it would have long lasting consequences for the rest of my life.

The worst part is, it really did not have to be a tradeoff. I could have had my cake and eaten it too. All I needed to have done was allocate 25% more time on my academics and skipped out on a few parties and I could have had Adam like scores or better. Although my life ultimately turned out just fine, this was one of my biggest undergraduate regrets. I would ultimately achieve my dream, but it would take more time and at far greater expense than it needed to.

Chapter 10 - "Failure is the condiment that gives success its flavors" - Truman Capote

As I endeavored to right the wrongs of my academic career, by this time, separation had begun to take its toll on Kristen and I. Although she had transferred from West Chester to Kean University nearby in Union, NJ for her sophomore year and we were able to see one another more, we still had lives that were often separate from one another. Still, we stayed the course, going through alternating periods when we felt for one another as we did in high school and times when we felt disconnected and growing apart.

During one particular heart breaking time for me, Kristen told me that she thought it best that we separated for a while to evaluate our true feelings for one another. The truth, I later found out, was that Kristen was seeing someone else. Although things had not been great between us, it was still a very tough pill to swallow that my high school sweetheart was seeing another man.

Still, I gave her the space and the time she asked for and spent most of my time in my off campus apartment in Montclair with my two roommates, all three of us enrolled in summer classes. One day my roommate, Mike, (the same Mike from freshman year who ended up being my roommate and among my closest friends throughout college) was browsing through the newspaper and stumbled across the classified section where he saw an advertisement for Labrador Retriever puppies for sale.

Spending such little time back home in Clark, I had not seen much of Stanley by this time. He was the family dog anyway and a senior aged dog at this point and I would not take him with me up to school. I missed having the unconditional love of a pet and with what I was going through with Kristen, I really could have uses some unconditional love in my life.

On impulse, I picked up the phone and called the number from the advertisement and the breeder told me she still had several puppies left, males and females in black, yellow, and chocolate. My other roommate Charlie and I headed right over to check them out.

Upon entering the home, we were inundated with 12 week old Labrador puppies, mauling us with affection. They were all so beautiful and playful, but one was a little bit shy and stayed outside of the fray. With a little coaxing, she came over to sniff me and rather than jump all over me like the others, she climbed into my lap, curled up and laid her head down.

She was a yellow Lab but different from the other yellow puppies in the litter. Instead of having brown eyes and a black nose like most yellow Labs have, she had hazel green eyes with a brown, liver colored nose. This is a rare recessive trait expressed in some yellow Labrador Retrievers called the "Dudley" variation. Of course at the time I did not know that, I knew only that she was a stunning puppy and I loved her temperament. I wrote the $500 check, named her Tiffany (I am not sure why, but that name just came to me instantly), and Charlie, Tiffany and I proceeded straight to Petsmart to get the supplies we needed for our house's new puppy.

Tiffany was an absolute joy right from the outset. She nearly trained herself and was the center of attention of our apartment. She was never wanting for attention with at least one of us usually around to take out to potty, play with her, walk her and feed her. She may have been my puppy, but in that first year, she had three dads and we doted on her endlessly. Having the responsibility for and the love of my own dog, the first that was not a Welton family dog but completely my own, was just what the doctor ordered. I focused on school, my job at the veterinary clinic, and raising my new puppy.

Months went by without any contact from Kristen and I was at peace with it. I had even started dating someone else and had really started to move on without her. My roommates and other friends noticed how happy I was and they were happy for me. One of my more hilariously cynical friends Rich, however, joked that females have a 6th sense that tells them when their ex has moved on, that is the moment that they call.

Rich as I said was hilarious and I just laughed it off, but true to his prediction, I came home one day to check my messages and there was a message from none other than Kristen telling me that she was thinking of me and was reaching out to catch up and see how I was doing. My roommates always liked Kristen, but having witnessed firsthand how hard it was for me to get over her, they warned me not to call her back.

Not wanting to risk missing Kristen all over again, I took their advice and did not call. Then she left a second message, and then a third. At this point, I was legitimately concerned that she may have a familial issue or other personal problem she needed to talk to me about. She was in her heart a very good person and I could not deny that I played some role in our separation. I did not wish to see her hurting if she just needed a familiar and trusted voice to listen to whatever she may have been going through. So I called.

As it turned out, Kristen was not going through any personal crisis; she just simply missed me and wanted to see me. I told her that it was very hard for me to move on and that I did not want to have to go back to that place where I had to get over her again. I sincerely wished her well and said goodbye.

Exactly one hour after I had hung up the phone with her, she showed up at my apartment, having driven up to Montclair all the way from her parent's house in Scotch Plains (about a 40 minute drive). When I answered the door, she was both pleasantly surprised but sad to see I had a 6 month old Lab puppy. She loved animals as much as I do, but her sadness stemmed from the fact that I had adopted a dog months ago and she played no role in it or even knew anything about it.

She asked me to come out to her car to talk to have some privacy away from the roommates. She sat in the driver's seat and I sat in the passenger seat as she poured her heart out to me. She had not really ended up feeling the spark with the new guy that she had with me for all of our years together. Sometimes it takes living without a person to really appreciate them and I could not say that a part of me felt the same. Still, I could not shake off the hurt I felt when she left me for another guy and I told her frankly that I was seeing someone else and I really did not know what the future held with my feelings for each girl.

Undeterred, Kristen kept calling and I did not really mind. I was torn between the happiness I had found with a wonderful new girl I was seeing since my break up with Kristen and so many years of love and companionship I had enjoyed with my high school sweetheart. I thus continued chatting with Kristen, would meet up with her every time I was back in Clark to see my family, and she would come up to see me in Montclair. Little by little, we were back in one in another's lives, happy and grateful to have one another exclusively again.

Kristen also got to know my beloved puppy Tiffany and they took to one another quite readily. As I previously stated, Kristen was an animal lover and she had always lived vicariously through my pets since she could never have her own (her step father was allergic to dogs and cats).

Through it all, Kristen and I through our ups and downs loved one another dearly and aside from our one rough patch, we managed to stay together for the most part throughout college, and had become very close with one another's families. It was well believed and hoped by both of our families that we would eventually one day get married.

I especially had a good relationship with Kristen's mother to whom I did not sugar coat the fact that I was probably playing academic catch up too late to have a shot at getting into veterinary school. One day, she told me about her supervisor that was leaving her company to take a job in the office of admissions at a veterinary school called Ross University, School of Veterinary Medicine.

The school was at the time owned by Yale University, had its administrative and admissions offices on the Upper West Side of New York City, but the school itself was located on the Caribbean island of St. Kitts (one of the Leeward Islands in the British West Indies). While the roughly 3 year equivalent of preclinical study was completed on the island, the school would then place students at one of the stateside veterinary college teaching hospitals for one year of clinical training.

As I looked into the school, I learned that they were known for accepting students that were on the bubble for acceptance into one of the 27 US based veterinary schools. The Ross University curriculum was rigorous and ruthless. They saw their mission as

54

being the second and last chance for students that still had the wherewithal to not give up on their dreams to one day become a practicing veterinarian. While they would lower their admission standard slightly, they would mercilessly weed out students.

Students who failed even one class would fall back into the class behind them to repeat the entire semester. A student who failed a second time would have to submit an appeal to the academic board for reinstatement for consideration to be allowed to repeat again. A third fail resulted in dismissal from the university. What's more, Ross University did not permit students to get D's, so a failing grade was anything below 70%

This was a huge ray of hope for me, as I not only saw a way forward in the event that it was too little too late to be accepted to a US based school, but I was also excited at the prospect of living in the West Indies for a few years. I made an appointment with my advisor, biochemistry department head, Dr. Delaney, to discuss this potential path.

Dr. Delaney unfortunately could not be of much assistance, as most biochemistry students generally were not applying to medical or veterinary school and were more likely headed to enter research internships or go on to earn PHD's. She referred me to an advisor in the biology department that served to advise aspiring veterinarians in the science department.

I will simply call her Dr. S, as I do not hold her in very high regard since our meeting. At first friendly and receptive, as soon as I brought up Ross University, her demeanor instantly changed and she became dismissive and cynical. She advised me that going there would be a waste of time and money, as graduating from there, I would have a very hard time getting licensed to practice in the US, and even if I did, no one would hire me.

I was considering going on to point out information that I had gathered quite to the contrary of her advice, but sensing that my mere presence was annoying her by that point, I refrained, thanked Dr. S for her time, and left. Needless to say, I was disappointed and felt like I was back to square one.

That summer, one of my good friends' brothers had just graduated from Chiropractic School and was setting up his own practice in our home town. My friend was also in the process of applying to Life College of Chiropractic to follow in big brother's footsteps.

At the time, I was nursing various injuries I had sustained in my years of playing college lacrosse. When my friend's brother, Dr. Jay Paris, opened his practice over the summer break between my junior and senior years, I spent a great deal of time with him in his practice learning about chiropractic and its ability to heal the body without the side effects of medication.

As my injuries healed and my posture improved, with the ever-passionate Jay constantly educating me about chiropractic, I became very interested and could imagine myself potentially making a living at this as well. What's more, his younger brother Brian who was my lacrosse teammate and childhood buddy, was on his way to becoming a chiropractor as well and I thought about how cool it would be to go to graduate school with a lifelong friend.

As my parents became aware of my interest in chiropractic, they too sought out the services of Dr. Jay and enjoyed the benefits of his expertise. They had been patients of chiropractors in the past, but really embraced the innovation that newly graduated young Dr. Jay brought to the profession.

However, when it came to my embracing of chiropractic as a possible career choice for me, they politely nodded but never really gave me the enthusiastic response I was accustomed to when they truly supported an endeavor of mine. I was so young and sure of myself that I never really bothered to ask why.

It would be a family vacation that summer to New England and my father that would that would steer me back to on the path of veterinary medicine.

Chapter 11 - "It's never too late to be what you might have been." - George Eliot

Kristen had worked a few summers as a nanny for the children of a fairly well to do family that spent long periods of their summers on the island of Block Island, a picturesque island off the coast of Rhode Island. One summer in our early college years, the family had suggested that Kristen and I drive to New London, Connecticut to park our car and take our bikes on the ferry to spend a week with them in their rental house on the island. It cost at the time only $2.50 to bring your bike on the ferry and the island was so small that just about everywhere was quite reachable by bike with amazing views and a fresh sea breeze to grace one's journey. It also meant a cheap vacation for a couple of broke college kids.

The week we spent there was magical, warm and sunny during the day as we toured the island by bike, visited overlooks of bluffs over 100 feet high, and toured incredible historical landmarks. In the evenings, the weather would be a bit more brisk and we would put on hoodies and ride our bikes into town, have dinner and walk around the festive harbor. It was the perfect combination of young love in a beautiful, historical, and remote setting.

Block Island to this day remains among my favorite places I have visited in my life. In the summer of 1996 while the Welton family contemplated where we would vacation, Kristen and I thought it would be a good idea to suggest we go back to Block Island, as well as visit three other more commonly known New England tourist destinations, the islands of of Nantucket and Martha's Vineyard; then to Cape Cod to explore the land of the Kennedy's and finally Bar Harbor Maine.

On the drive up from NJ, I was driving and my Dad was in the front passenger seat of my Ford Explorer. The ladies - my Mom, Kristen, and little sister Leslie - were in the back seat lost in their own conversation. It was at that time my Dad brought up what he thought about my consideration of chiropractic as a career.

My Dad respected the profession and saw value in it, himself a patient of my friend Dr. Jay Paris. He noted that it is a noble career pursuit for many people...but not for me.

He shared with me that he had no doubt that I would make a fine chiropractor and would help many people. However, he felt strongly that knowing my passion for the field of veterinary medicine that I would always live with the regret of giving up on my dream.

I shared with him my conversation with Dr. S, that the path forward for me at this point seemed an impossible one, and that I had made my bed and need to now make the best of the consequences. My Dad answered in no uncertain terms that this was unacceptable, that without mitigating circumstances like having children to feed or even being married, that there was nothing keeping me from taking the time to find a way to fulfill my dream. He told me if I wanted it badly enough, I would find way or risk living with regret for the rest of my life.

I took his words to heart. I told my Dad that when I returned to school in the fall for my final year, I would look into what I had to do to find my way to veterinary school.

I began by registering to take the Graduate Record Exam (GRE), the standardized testing that veterinary and other graduate programs used to evaluate applicants. I ultimately scored in the top 10% of all students who took the GRE that year. Good start!

That winter break, rather than just screw around with my high school buddies back home, I volunteered at a stable to gain large animal husbandry experience and gain a recommendation from the stable manager. This would broaden my animal experience and add to the large number of hours I had already compiled working part time at the small animal veterinary hospital through college.

I kept my grades up in my final year of school, but by this point, bringing up the GPA was very difficult and I still hovered in the 3.3-3.4 range. I would have to rely on my experience, my strong GRE scores, and hopefully kill the interviews, that is, if I was even granted any.

As luck would have it, I befriended a student from Barbados named Simmy in my Instrumental Biochemistry lab class just before I was to send out my veterinary school applications, and we became lab partners. I learned that he had been accepted to Ross University School of Medicine (the sister medical school to Ross University School of Veterinary Medicine). Surprised to hear this after my past conversation with Dr. S about what a waste of time and money Ross University would be, I shared the conversation I had with Dr. S with Simmy and he started laughing.

He told me that Dr. S is a miserable hag who seemingly hated students. Apparently she was the advisor for premedical students as well and that this was her general reputation; that is, a killer of dreams when students did not fit the particular mold she deemed fit for a career in veterinary or human medicine. Understanding the kind of person Dr. S was, Simmy took it upon himself to research the school more intently, even visit their administrative and admissions offices in New York

City. They even gave him alumni contacts practicing in our area for him to contact and share their experience.

He learned that the education was top notch with tenured and respected US and Canadian based professors being attracted to teaching at Ross because as a pure teaching institution, there were no "publish or perish" pressures placed on professors to maintain their tenure. Being able to just teach combined with good pay and an opportunity to live in the Caribbean attracted top teaching talent.

There were many practicing Ross graduate doctors all over the country in both human and veterinary medicine, proving that Dr. S was completely wrong about the inability to get a job post-graduation. The only extra wrinkle that Ross graduates had to go through with their technical consideration by the state medical and veterinary boards as foreign veterinary graduates (with the exception of New York that waved that consideration in light of Ross grads having to complete their final year of clinical training at accredited teaching hospitals in the United States).

For a Ross graduate to be licensed to practice in the US with the exception of NY, in addition to passing the national board exams, Ross graduates also had to take a 3 day hands on practical test called the Clinical Proficiency Exam (CPE). It added a layer of complication and expense (at the time, the test cost $2000 to take), but certainly not a deal breaker for a passionate and motivated veterinary candidate.

Thus, while I knew that state side veterinary school would be a long shot for me, I felt that should Ross University accept me, Dr. S's opinion notwithstanding, I knew it was a viable option for me. I would include an application to Ross U as well in the veterinary school application process.

Ultimately a person has to find his or her way, but my talk with my Dad changed my life. It would always stay with me how profoundly the impact a parent that loves you and believes in you could have. I left my heart to heart with my Dad with a new determination because he had no doubt in his mind that as long as I wanted it badly enough and stayed the course; I would one day be a doctor of veterinary medicine!

Chapter 12 - "At the moment of truth there are either reasons
or results" - Chuck Yeager

By the fall of 1997, I still had some credits to finish up to
graduate and all my vet school applications were out. My
eligibility for lacrosse was over and at the end of the 1996
graduation year (the year I should have graduated had I finished
in 4 years) I still had 10 credits to finish up my biochemistry
degree. Since the earliest I could matriculate into a veterinary
class should I gain acceptance was fall 1998, I decided to stretch
out the credits as a part time student and use my extra free
time to increase my hours working at the veterinary clinic; and
graduate with the class of 1997.

Thus, I went on about my life preparing to put my college years
behind me and trying not to stress about the vet school
applications. I was so determined at this point that I was going
to be a veterinarian one day, I was fully prepared to apply again
for entrance into 1999 should it not work out this time around.
I had learned from young veterinarians I worked with at the
clinic, that vet schools liked that kind of persistence and it was
not unusual to have vet school classmates that had applied 2
and 3 times before getting accepted.

In winter of early 1998, one letter came after another from the
schools I had applied to thanking me for my application but
regretfully informing me that I did not meet the requirements
for their doctor of veterinary medicine programs at this time. I
was not even granted an interview for one of the state side
schools I had applied to.

There were still 1 or 2 stateside applications that I still had yet
to hear from when the Ross University letter arrived. They had
granted me an interview at their New York City admissions

office. I promptly called the office and made my appointment, then went right to the mall to buy a suit for the interview.

I arrived to the office and saw there were three other applicants awaiting their interviews. They began by ushering us into a boardroom where the director of admissions gave a slideshow with a presentation of the overview of the curriculum, expectations they had of students, and a brief history, culture, and government lesson on the island of of St. Kitts, the larger island of the commonwealth of St Kitts & Nevis that housed the country's main port and capital city of Basseterre.

One by one, the candidates were called in to the office of our respective assigned admissions officer. Mine was a man about in his late thirties that had a friendly disposition. He asked me questions about details of my application, why I selected biochemistry as a major and he was especially curious about my college lacrosse career (much to my pleasant surprise, he had played lacrosse in high school).

The admissions officer told me he was impressed with my GRE scores and work experience but noted that my grade point average was borderline, difficult major notwithstanding. However, he wanted to be clear that while grades were important, Ross University considers the entire candidate, not just major, GRE scores, and GPA. He went on that their job as Ross U admissions officers is to be as certain as possible that a candidate would be able withstand a rigorous curriculum while living a foreign country (that outside of the tourist sector was essentially third world), be moved again stateside for his/her clinical year, and pass both national boards and the 3 day long Clinical Proficiency Examination for foreign veterinary graduates.

He then told me that my admission would largely depend on my answer to the following question, "Why do you want to be a veterinarian?" No pressure, right?! He told me that by virtue of his job as an objective and impartial evaluator the he could not offer me advice or guidance how to answer, other than offering that professing my love of animals as a main reason was not a good answer. He noted that the world is full of people who love animals but they may not possess the intelligence, discipline, or stomach for a career in veterinary medicine.

I took a moment to collect my thoughts and recalled my answer to the admissions officer when he asked me why I opted for biochemistry as a major when I could have chosen any number of less challenging science majors that would have qualified me to apply for veterinary school. I told him that biology and zoology were interesting but to me were little more than academic regurgitation. I chose biochemistry because I wanted to learn about the origins of life and how it worked at the molecular level from metabolic reactions and tissue building, to DNA and RNA synthesis and replication. Biochemistry would provide me a strong foundation for understanding disease and medicine at the cell and molecular level.

Here was my answer to why I wanted to be a veterinarian:

At the risk of sounding cliche, I cannot separate my love of animals from the answer as to why I want to be a veterinarian. A fascination with, respect for, and empathy for animals is something intrinsic in me and in large measure defines me as a person. Providing relief for animals when sick or injured through my skill as a healer and providing them the mercy of humane euthanasia when their degree of illness or injury is beyond the scope of medicine to help them would fulfill this passion.

I was also born with a passion for science and how the world and especially life works. Science not only provides these answers but it does so objectively, quantitatively, and without opinion. Feelings or belief systems have no place in science, only facts based on tangible evidence and research.

Veterinary medicine not only would provide me with the gratification of helping animals, but it is also an application of the scientific method. Medical history, physical examination, and lab data lead us to the diagnoses necessary to best treat the patient and the treatments available to us to treat disease come from extensive research and clinical trials.

Applied science that benefits animals is why I not only want to be a veterinarian, but why I am absolutely certain that I will be an excellent veterinarian.

Throughout my answer to his question, the admissions officer sat stone faced with no expression or even a nod or shake of the head. However, after my last sentence, I was fairly positive that I saw the hint of a smile form at the corners of his mouth. With that, he thanked me for coming in and told me I will be receiving a letter with the school's answer in 1-2 weeks.

I felt good about the interview and knew that in the past year, I had done everything I could to re-focus and pursue my dream just as my father had encouraged me to do. I cannot say that I was not anxious about getting into veterinary school this year, for I was ready to get on with my life with my now clearly defined goal and purpose. On the other hand, I felt at peace and whatever resulted from my interview and the remaining applications left to come, I would take it in stride and take the next step, whatever that may be.

Chapter 13 - "You raze the old to raise the new" - *Justina Chen*

Exactly 10 days after my Ross U interview, my letter (more like a folder thick with contents - usually a good sign) arrived. I did not open it right away, but left it on my living room coffee table and stared at it for a bit. When I opened it and read the letter on top, literally jumped for joy as I saw the first word of the first paragraph of the letter, "Congratulations!"

As I read on, I barely noticed that the acceptance class was not fall 1998, but winter of 1999. Ross U operates in trimesters (although students still call them semesters) that operated year round through the summer as well. That is why students got 3 years equivalent of preclinical training in 2 ½ years that they were on the island (provided they did not fail back into other classes).

I really did not care about this slight delay, as it would give me more time to get my affairs in order, continue working and put away more money, and in the grand scheme, what was another 4 months in the grand scheme of things?

Once I knew I was accepted to Ross U, even if I was offered interviews at the remaining veterinary schools I had not yet heard back from, I would turn down the interviews and attend Ross. I was so excited about the prospect of not only learning veterinary medicine and working toward my doctorate, but doing so while living on a Caribbean island! I felt my destiny pulling me there, as if fate had intended for me to live in St Kitts and train at Ross University all along.

Knowing that it would be roughly 11 months until I would be departing for St Kitts, my buddy Steve had asked me to take the summer to tour Europe with him. He had just graduated

University of Maryland and as a graduation gift, his parents offered to finance a backpacking tour of Europe.

As my last summer in NJ and in the United States for that matter for a while, I told Steve that I was reluctant to spend my entire last summer on another continent instead of among friends, family, and Kristen. Ever the adventurous spirit, Steve had determined that even if I did not join him, he would backpack around Europe on his own (I could write an entire book about my friend Steve, perhaps my next one!). He asked if I would compromise and meet him for 2 weeks on the Spain and France leg of his tour which I found to be the perfect compromise. We booked and paid for our respective trips and I was all set to meet him in Barcelona, Spain in the last 2 weeks of July.

Knowing this would be the last summer I would spend with my network of college and high school friends for a while, I also got in on a summer house rental with a bunch of other guys at the Jersey Shore in Belmar. Kristen and her friends got a rental house for the summer in nearby Manasquan so we would be able to see one another often.

Shortly after having made all of these plans and paid for them (the shore house and flights to Europe and back), I got a call from the Ross University Office of Admissions. I was informed that a spot had opened up for the fall class of 1998 and I was being offered the slot if I wanted to start school earlier that the original winter class of 1999 I had gotten accepted for.

On one hand I thought, emphatically yes! On the other hand, I had made these summer plans and had not yet begun to fully delve into my preparations to leave for school. I still needed to renew my passport, apply to St Kitts for my student visa, purchase all of the required items (dissection kit, microscope, scrubs, books, etc.), and apply for student loans. I also needed to sell my truck. As all of this flew through my head in a nanosecond, I simply replied to the admissions officer, "Sure."

My last summer spending my weekends at the Jersey Shore was a pretty typical Jersey Shore experience: beach, surfing, beer pong, bars, and late night gorging on boardwalk pizza. Tiffany was our house mascot and was very doted on by all my friends. She was so good that she did not ever need a leash, just stayed at my side at all times.

The house we rented was very cool with apartments behind us and on either side of the house, we shared on big courtyard with other college aged renters, so it was one big party 24/7. We had a big baby pool that we lounged in when we tired of the beach and Tiffany never hesitated to wade in with us. It was such carefree and unbridled fun with the people I enjoyed the most.

During the week, I split time working at the vet clinic and making all of the aforementioned preparations for school. The school had let me know soon enough that with haste, I could get it all done. I ultimately decided not to sell my SUV, as I would need a car when I got back in 2 ½ years to take to whatever school I got placed and would not need the aggravation and added expense of having to buy a car. My parents would look after it at their home and use it occasionally so it would not sit idle and decay..

The Europe trip in late July came quickly. As planned, I met Steve in Barcelona at the airport. By this time, Steve had been traipsing all over Europe by himself and was a seasoned international traveler. I will not get into too much detail about the specifics of our trip, but it was an amazing 2 weeks. We were two 24 year old childhood friends, how could it not be epic?

After spending a week in Spain, we travelled by overnight train to Nice in the south of France. Early in our week there, we took a taxi to Monte Carlo and as luck would have it, we won $2500 playing blackjack. Needless to say, we spent the week living pretty high on the hog!

After a great 2 weeks in Europe with my childhood best friend, I left Steve in Nice flying back home from the airport there, and he continued on his own to see the rest of the European continent that he had not yet travelled to.

When I returned, there were only a few weeks of summer left and I resumed my routine of working and making preparations to leave the country, while spending the weekends at the shore house with my friends and Kristen.

One night, I was watching TV and St Kitts was a featured story on the World Nightly News on ABC. There was a drug kingpin operating out of Miami that had disappeared with law enforcement hot on his tail, years later to have been discovered by the FBI, living and continuing his trade on the Island of St. Kitts in the summer of 1998. He went by the name "Little Nut," but his real name was Chris Miller.

As the FBI was petitioning the government of St. Kitts and Nevis to allow extradition of Miller back to the United States, Little Nut declared that if they did not back off, he and his henchmen on the island would start executing American veterinary students studying at Ross University.

I could not believe it. How could it be possible that on this obscure little island that I had previously never heard of and only weeks from travelling to live and study there, an international incident reported on all the major news networks was occurring?

Naturally I was concerned, but my parents were absolutely mortified at the thought of me going there under these circumstances. I called the school and made inquiries as to how real the danger was and the school stated that Chris Miller was making empty threats he could not carry out with constant police surveillance on him and increased security at the school in light of the threat. Despite downplaying the threat, they offered the option to defer to the winter 1999 semester, that hopefully by then there would be a resolution to this problem.

After careful consideration and discussion with my parents, I decided I was going. To make herself feel better, my Mom asked my older brother to travel with me to St. Kitts to spend my first week on the island to help me acclimate to living abroad and also help me make sensible decisions if the Little Nut thing became evidently dangerous (despite the fact that my brother was really no more sensible than I was!).

On one hand, I was a little disappointed that my Mom did not trust her 24 year old college graduate to adjust and stay safe. On the other hand, my brother Ernie and I had always been close and I welcomed his company to be with me during the first couple of weeks of my new life abroad.

The night before my departure, I had all the possessions I would be taking with me for the next 2 ½ years packed in 2 suitcases. Naturally, I spent the evening with Kristen. It was early September and this would be the last I would see her until

Christmas. There was still no social media by this time and the cost to talk on the phone internationally was $3 plus per minute. We agreed we would talk once a week for 15 minutes and alternate who made the call to share in the cost.

Even though this would be a much farther and longer separation than when we had departed to college as high school sweethearts, we handled it much better. We were both more mature, had endured separation by our own volition, and both had a feeling that if we were meant to remain together, so it would be. If not, that was to be what fate had in store for us.

Still, there were some tears. We had spent the last 7 plus years together, had essentially grown together from high school teens to young adults. We were both college graduates and I was on my way to starting my doctorate. Kristen was well into her career as a school teacher. Much had changed since we had met in high school, yet the fact that we were one another's first loves connected us on a deep level.

Chapter 14 - "We're not in Kansas anymore Toto." - *Dorothy, Wizard of Oz*

At the time, the Royal St. Kitts International Airport was so small that only small propeller planes could land there. People travelling to St Kitts would typically connect in Puerto Rico and board a small puddle jumper type prop plane to the island.

I recall as we were making our approach to the island, it reminded me of a TV show I grew up watching called "Fantasy Island," a show about a picturesque island of lush green mountains and cascading waterfalls; where each episode, people with all manners of personal issues and crises would go to work through them and dreams would come true (or epiphanies had) with the help of the magical beauty of the island and the resort's enigmatic host Mr. Roarke and his little assistant Tattoo.

Like Fantasy Island, the Island of St. Kitts had several lush green mountains but one in particular dominated the island, a dormant, nearly 4000 ft volcano called Mount Liamuiga. We landed and as we went through baggage claim and later customs, we got our first introduction to Caribbean culture. We were the only flight that had come in at the time, a max of 20 people. Yet, the process took seemingly forever.

Kittitians as the native citizens of St Kitts are called, had little sense of urgency or hurry. You could be standing next in line and an attendant may continue in a task and not acknowledge your presence for several minutes. Once attended to, they were pleasant and friendly enough, but they really took their time and gave the impression that they were detached and dismissive.

Apparently, this was quite typical. A representative from the school was to meet us at the airport (a few incoming freshmen were on the flight and the rep had our flight numbers) but was not there as we waited for her at the arrivals section of the airport. She apologized and told us that she was late because she got stuck behind a sugar cane tractor on her way. Knowing how slow the airport staff was, she was half thinking her lateness would not have mattered.

On than vane, the rep advised us to always try to remember to give at least 45 minutes leeway to arrive on time for class or any other planned engagement because with only 2 lane roads leading everywhere (with no center markers I might add), a sugar cane tractor could delay you for a long time depending on where it may be headed (most of the interior of the island was sugar cane fields, a very important cash crop at the time in St. Kitts).

I also met my first friend on the island while on line at customs, a very friendly and pretty young lady named Cara. Cara was interesting in many ways, but what really intrigued me the most at the time was that this was my first real exposure to a person from the Deep South. Cara was technically from the interior of Florida, not the Florida that tourists that travel to in Orlando and the coasts see, but the part that is essentially very much and extension of the Deep South.

With the school headquarters located in NYC, I really did not anticipate this. As it turned out, there were field offices of admissions in Miami, California, and the Midwest for the school to have the opportunity to interview students from across the country without too much travel burden. The center in Miami also enabled veterinary candidates from Puerto Rico to apply for admission as well.

Talking to Cara was really familiar and normal at first just connecting with a fellow American in a foreign country very different from ours, but it did not take long to gain the realization of how so very different cultures existed within my own country! I was floored!

This is no affront to Cara whatsoever, as I am very certain that as her first real experience with a "Yankee," she was just as surprised as I was about the differences. She was a highly intelligent, beautiful young lady who is still a beautiful and very successful mother, wife, and veterinarian who I remain friends with to this day.

On my first day in the group I was being picked up, Cara ended up being the first of an interesting diversity of people I was to have in my class. There was a guy despite the 99 degree heat and 100% humidity that was dressed in a cowboys hat, long sleeve button up shirt, Wrangler jeans with a huge belt buckle, and cowboy boots (not to mention, he wore a big, bushy beard). His name was Chuck and I asked him if he was hot and despite clearly sweating he said that coming from the interior of Georgia, he was quite comfortable dressed in his horse ranch attire, calling his jeans his "in town britches.".

There was Sam from Washington State, arriving with nothing but a guitar case and a hiking type backpack slung on his back with long hair, a weathered tie dye t-shirt, cutoff jeans, and sporting a 3 day scruff.

The one in the group that was most familiar to me despite meeting him just for the first time was Peter from Long Island,

NY. Culturally, NJ and lower NY are quite similar and I played college lacrosse with Long Island guys, so talking with Peter came quite naturally.

There was of course my travelling companion, my older brother Ernie. I have to admit, it was comforting to have him with me in this early introduction to my life as a veterinary student in a foreign country meeting fellow American students, many of which were far different than me. On the flip side, this was as much a fun trip for my brother as it was a trip to help little brother acclimate to his new home.

Our school representative told us she would drive us to our respective hotels, suggested that we unpack and relax, take in the culture, and enjoy the raw beauty of the island for the day. She would take us to available rental properties the next morning to find housing well in advance of our first incoming student orientation.

My brother and I had booked our hotel stay at a beautiful, all inclusive beach resort called the Jack Tarr Resort. Adjacent to the resort was the Royal St Kitts Casino, and there was Karaoke Night in the hotel's night club every evening. "All inclusive" included both unlimited food and open bar, so we were pretty well set up.

We of course partook in the hotel's amenities and the next morning when the school representative arrived to take us out with other students to check out housing, we were both pretty mercilessly hung-over. This made for a great day cooped up in a van driving through the winding stop and go through St Kitts traffic looking at different housing options.

My goal primarily was to remain in the main tourist area, a region called Frigate Bay. Around the school, it was a fairly remote area with no swimming beaches or entertainment and it was known to be an area where breaks-ins into residences and theft were more common. Because of all the resorts, in a country with a fairly primitive power grid that commonly lost power often for no apparent reason, Frigate Bay was always prioritized to get the power back online (this would prove extremely important later on!).

If I could avoid it, I really did not wish to take on a roommate, yet being a very social person, I wanted to be in a community where there were other students around. The school representative found me a particularly appealing option of a studio apartment attached to the back of a house that housed 4 veterinary students in second semester. They were all very friendly and the property was nice, sitting on the side of a mountain overlooking Frigate Bay with a view of the Caribbean Sea on one side and the Atlantic Ocean on the other. However, there was one red flag and probably the reason the apartment had not been rented out in a while: there was no air conditioning!

There were three windows available that would fit a window unit air conditioner, so I asked if there was an electronics or hardware store where I could purchase one. There was not, but the school rep told me that she knew of several students that had their parents ship them window units from the US that they later sold to new incoming students when they graduated.

The price was also unbelievable, only $400 per month. In my brother's mind it was settled and this was our ticket to be done with home hunting and back to the resort in time for happy hour, dinner, and casino time. He said he would have my parents buy me an air conditioner ASAP and have it shipped to St Kitts to solve my issue in no time. His logic made enough sense to me so I took the apartment and went back to the resort with my brother.

The next order of business the next day was to purchase a car. Cars on the isolated little island of St Kitts were at the time in finite supply, so the selection was not great and the cars were subsequently terribly overpriced. Most students bought epic jalopies that people would not likely be able to give away back in the US, often from other students that were graduating and looking to recoup the money they invested in their temporary vehicle they owned during their time on the island. Student cars were jokingly called "Ross-mobiles," and never ceased to be a source of humor for the students.

My brother and I went to a used car lot in the capital city of Basseterre and perused the humorous selection. The one I settled on was a 12 year old Nissan Sentra that had been recently traded in by a Rastafarian that had some pretty interesting Rastafarian decor in the car. It was a burgundy car with windows tinted in limousine black with a big white tiger etched onto the rear windshield. The steering wheel and seats were upholstered with a furry leopard covering that retained the unmistakable smell of marijuana. I paid $3500 for the car that was quite special even among some of the most legendary Ross-mobiles. But unlike the majority of other Ross-mobiles, it had functioning air conditioning!

Driving the car back to the hotel was rather interesting. Having previously been a British Commonwealth, St Kitts cars were set up with the driver on the right side of the car and right of way was on left side of the road. Although I was rather surprised how quickly I eventually got used to it, it was a rather odd experience at first.

Two days later, it was time for my brother to fly back home to the US. I was sad to see him go but he was determined to return often having loved his first visit to St Kitts. There really was something rather alluring about the island and its simplicity, lacking major development with miles of unspoiled, undeveloped, empty beaches and everything being unique and authentic. It was very unlike some of the islands we had visited on cruise stops on family vacations with our parents that were beautiful but built out and heavily commercialized with even fast food chains on them. Thus, knowing I would see him again soon and with student orientation lurking the next day, I was ready and eager to get settled into my new place and prepare to start my new education.

After dropping off my brother I went back to the hotel to collect my things and pack my car for the 5 minute drive up to my new studio apartment. Upon entering, even well after dusk and a steady breeze, I realized I did not really fully understand the depths of the discomfort not having air conditioning would be like in early September in the Caribbean. It was stifling! But still, I knew that all I had to do was suck it up just long enough for my parents to send me a window unit air conditioner.

I unpacked and loaded my drawers and closet (as a young man, I did not pack a great deal with me) and proceeded to take a shower and prepare for bed. Within about 1 minute of starting the shower, a multitude of worms started oozing up and out of the shower drain and wriggling around the shower. Never having seen anything like this in my life, I was thoroughly freaked out, dried and dressed quickly, and knocked on the door of the second semester people living in the main house.

J.P. (a guy I would end up being friends with for the duration of my time in St Kitts) answered the door and I told him about what happened. He walked over and checked it out and told me he had heard about this happening in plumbing that had not been used in a while but had never actually seen it...although, he shared my disgust in seeing it.

I thanked J.P., packed up all my things, and drove back down to the Jack Tarr Resort; thankfully they had a vacancy and I checked back in. I promptly called the school rep about my experience in my new place and told her in no uncertain terms that I needed a new place. In an amazing twist of fate, she told me she had the perfect place, as a fifth semester student - from NJ of all places - needed a roommate stat, since his previous roommate suddenly and abruptly moved out (more on this in a moment). What's more, it was a two bedroom condominium in a complex that was just walking distance from the Jack Tarr Resort, a 200 yard walk from the Atlantic Ocean, ¼ mile walk to the Caribbean Sea, with a nice pool and a restaurant right next door. It was full of predominantly veterinary students and I learned later that it was nicknamed "Melrose Place" after a popular drama in the 1990's about young professionals that lived in a similar looking condo complex in L.A. Another bonus, rent included weekly housekeeping service!

I hit it off very well with my new roommate Ben. He was happy to have an instant replacement roommate to share in the rent after being greeted to his new semester suddenly having no roommate, and I was thrilled to be moving into a nice place without worms oozing up through the drains. My room had its own outside entrance and its own bathroom, so having a roommate in this setting I did not think would cramp my style much at all. Naturally curious about the sudden departure of the previous roommate's, I asked Ben what had happened and he told me that his previous roommate's girlfriend from college that came with him to St Kitts after both getting accepted to school had left him for another male student and moved in with him directly upstairs. Tormented by the fact that he could hear his ex-girlfriend making love with the new boyfriend just above his bedroom nightly, he could not take it anymore and secured new housing unbeknownst to Ben. My goodness, you cannot make this stuff up!

Now settled and feeling somewhat stable in my new home in my new country as I was about to start in my new school the next day, I quickly got settled, took a shower (no worms this time) and drifted off into a deep, dreamless sleep.

Chapter 15 - "Change can be scary, but do you know what's scarier? Allowing fear to stop you from growing, evolving, and progressing" - *Mandy Hale*

I awoke 2 hours before orientation was to begin at school heeding the advice of the school rep to always leave a 45 minute cushion to get to school to avoid being late in the event of getting stuck behind a sugar cane tractor. I gave myself a full hour on the morning of orientation and learned that the drive to school under normal circumstances was 15 minutes, subsequently arriving 45 minutes early to a virtually empty parking lot.

Remember I told you about that drug dealer on the island that was threatening to execute US veterinary students if the US Justice Department continued to push for extradition; and the school assured incoming students that on campus security would be beefed up? Well upon arrival, I was curious as to what security looked like before the threats because all I saw was one unarmed Kittitian lady in a security outfit sitting in a booth that waved me on into the parking lot. I was to learn later that day that the drug dealer named Little Nut lived in a neighborhood called Mattingly that was only a ¼ mile up the road from the school.

Nonetheless, I was too excited and nervous to really give it much thought and having arrived so early I was able to tour the campus and was captivated with what I saw. The school campus sat on a fairly high elevation on the side of a mountain that ended abruptly at a steep cliff toward the Caribbean Sea. Thus, the parking lots were arranged in several levels, as was the campus with each level connected by stairs. The lowest level was the classrooms where lectures and histology (microscopic anatomy) labs were held. The next level up was the anatomy lab , followed by faculty offices and the top level was the teaching hospital, library, computer center, bookstore, student lounge, and cafeteria.

At every level of campus you had a breathtaking view of the aquamarine Caribbean Sea with the Island of St. Eustatius clearly visible to the west of campus. Eustatius was so close, you could even make out homes and buildings on the island.

The hour for orientation came and we all filed into a big lecture hall. I was amazed at the size of my class totaling 84. Orientation began with the school's Dean of Students Dr. Stanley Dennis speaking, a very stoic man who never smiled, and had a reputation for being an uncompromising major stickler for the rules. Dean Dennis held two veterinary specialty board certifications in pathology and theriogenology and had been hired as Dean of Ross University School of Veterinary Medicine following a distinguished career at the University of Queensland (Australia) College of Veterinary Medicine. This was no man to trifle with.

Dean Dennis went on to tell us that the faculty at Ross was tasked with preparing future generations of doctors and that they took that duty very seriously. That meant that professionalism and character was heavily weighed and lateness, poor attendance, showing disrespect toward professors and clinicians would not be tolerated.

Dean Dennis continued to state that everyone who was present was capable of completing the Ross University curriculum according to their admission standards but that many would fail nonetheless not be fully willing to accept the time and discipline it takes to absorb all of the information that was to be thrown at us. He asked us to look around to the people surrounding us and note that many will not be present in second semester having failed into the class behind us or just outright left the island.

Everything I had learned about Ross as I made inquiries was true. Dean Dennis confirmed that the failure policy was quite draconian at Ross University. The program had reputation for giving stateside bubble students a chance but once in the program would weed out many students leaving only the top echelon of students that would ultimately go on to stateside clinics, graduate and become working DVMs.

Students were not allowed to receive a D grade in any class. Thus, score below 70% was considered failing. What's more, if a student failed one class, he/she would be required to repeat the entire semester, including all of the other classes he/she passed, even if they were passed with all A's.

In the event of a second failure, a student would be referred to a faculty council that would determine if the student should be reinstated and given a third chance. A third failure was mandatory dismissal from the school.

Ultimately, out of a class that originally numbered 84, I graduated with a class of 38, only 33 of which were original first semester class members. If someone had told me then that I would be one of only 33 of 84 students left in my class to move on to clinics, I would have not felt very optimistic

The next speaker was the student government rep for the 7th semester, the final class before embarking on to clinics with an imminent departure from the island only 3 plus months away. He greeted us all with a smile and told us that he and his classmates were living proof that we too could make it. His main task was to show us a slideshow of telling us about some of the unique dangers of the island that we all needed to be wary of.

The first slide he put up was of a giant centipede next to a 12 inch ruler that was longer than the ruler with big menacing pinchers. He noted that these centipedes had a very venomous bite that caused severe pain and swelling the site of the bite, was known to even cause pain and swelling of an entire extremity, high fever, and in rare cases, death.

He went on to explain that centipedes were most commonly found in residences around the countryside like some of the neighborhoods near the school, but they crawl up through tiny cracks in foundations and were not uncommonly seen in the more high end condominiums of Frigate Bay (I was to stumble upon many during my time on the island but thankfully never got stung).

He next showed us an up close picture of a mosquito and strongly advised bug spray when outside at night. Among other diseases, mosquitoes of the Caribbean spread a very serious and potentially deadly viral disease called Dengue Fever. He cautioned it best to avoid contracting the disease to keep us out of the hospital that was perhaps as equally frightening as any condition that would put us in the hospital. The 7th semester student pointed out that outside the tourist areas and the port, the country of St Kitts and Nevis was essentially a third world country and its hospital very much reflected that. He concluded by telling us to find him in the student lounge if any of us were in need of a car (in 7th semester, preparing to leave the island in a few months, students are eager to sell their Ross mobiles).

Another speaker came out to tell us about the process to get our pets transported down to the island. As a rabies free island, they had a strict vaccination and rabies vaccine titer testing protocol that took three months so in an effort to get our pets down with us by second semester, he advised us to start the process with the island state veterinarian immediately (Tiffany at this time was staying with my parents back home awaiting her future trip to join me on the island).

Once all of the speaking was done, we were taken out by 7th semester student volunteers in groups of 10 to get a guided tour of the entire campus. By noon, we were directed to the bookstore to pick up all of our equipment and textbooks we had pre-purchased and dismissed with an invitation and directions to the 1st semester student welcome reception that was to take place at one of the resorts later that evening.

When I arrived at the party later that evening, I was rather amused that there were many upperclassmen present that had crashed the party. It was actually very nice to speak to people who were experienced in school and life on the island, see how at ease they were with it all, and it gave me more self-assurance that I would also assimilate to every aspect of it as they clearly did.

With regard to my own class, I was immediately taken back by the diversity of students from all over the continental United States, from my own Northeast urban/suburban region, to West Coasters, Rust Belt farmers, Southerners, and everyone in between. There was also a small number of Puerto Rican students as well.

In talking with many of these students, the differences among us were so clearly evident and while we all smiled and spoke politely with one another as we got acquainted, we all generally kind of gravitated toward those that were more like us. For me, it was the Northeastern Seaboard students from Maryland, NY, NJ, Connecticut, Massachusetts, etc.

It was to be incredible how much this would change as time passed and we all got to know one another well, over time realizing that there was far more we had in common than differences. In fact, the differences in the cultures and manners in which we all grew up over time made us even more interested in one another, less judgmental of one another's cultures, and awed by the fact that our country could produce such vastly different people under one flag.

One of the beauties of Ross University was that it was an almost all American student body, but was not a regional or state school. Instead, Ross was a school meant for all young Americans from corners of the country motivated by the dream of becoming veterinarians. That really was the main common bond that we all shared and in chasing that dream together we became ever closer with friendships that endure to this day more than 17 years later.

Chapter 16 - "Anyone who says they are not afraid at the time of a hurricane is either a fool or a liar, or a little bit of both" - *Anderson Cooper*

The first few weeks of school went by rather quickly and I had settled into my routine. School started every day at 8 AM and went until 4 PM with a one hour lunch break from Noon - 1 PM. After I arrived home at around 4:30 PM, I would exercise. Depending on the day, that would mean running a 5K around the roads of the tourist district where I lived, calisthenics on the beach (the Carribean beach was a 10 minute walk to the west, the Atlantic beach a 5 minute walk west from my condo), or swimming. I especially enjoyed my swimming days at the glassy calm Caribbean beach that was covered mostly by reef and gave me a great view of beautiful reef and sea creatures as I swam the coast.

After exercise, I would come home, get cleaned up and make dinner. After dinner, I would put in about 1-2 hours of studying and then walk over to my friend Nicole's place to hang out and chat, wind down, then return back to my place to turn in. I was advised by upperclassmen and faculty that routine is the key to success in veterinary school to keep up with the constant volume of piled on information to commit to memory, then step up the studying as midterms and finals approached.

On the weekends, unless there were pending lab practicals or tests, some students would go out. My favorite spot was a 1950's style bar and restaurant that had karaoke night every Saturday. It was also literally a 20 second walk from my condo and I became friends with the owners who were from, of all places, Southwest Jersey.

When I felt like playing pool or darts, we would go into Basseterre to a bar near the port called TOTT's (Tavern On The Town). After a particular grind of a week of tests and practicals, a group of students would sometimes splurge and get reservations at some of the fancy resorts to enjoy a gourmet dinner. Overall, life was rather pleasant.

Around mid-September, there was some grumbling around campus about some big storm that appeared could be headed toward St Kitts named George. Upperclassman and locals, paid it little worry, as they had seen storms threaten for years but the storms always seemed to veer in a direction away from the island. Even the locals paid it little worry even as it chugged along picking up strength and in the mid-Atlantic, still seeming to make a B line straight for our tiny island.

By the time George was a Category 3 storm and 5 days out, everyone really started to take notice. As it stood at that point, the eye wall was headed straight for us, but even if the storm veered, we were imminently going to get hit with a powerful part of the storm.

Ross called off school for the days that George was set to hit and advised all students to seek a hurricane shelter or seek refuge with classmates and friends that lived in newer, more reliable construction. The closest shelter to my condo was a resort a short walk away called Frigate Bay Resort. It was well protected because it sat at a high altitude on a mountain within a shallow, dormant volcanic crater shielding it from storm surge and wind generated projectiles.

Still, I was not inclined to check into a shelter and planned to ride the storm out in my condo. I had never experienced the wrath of a hurricane that was anything close to the size of

91

George, so I was the fool Anderson Cooper was referring to in the title of this chapter.

My friend Nicole who lived in the same condo complex as me, on the other hand, was no fool. She fully intended to go to the shelter and begged me to go with her. I thought she was being overly hysterical, but by this point, she was a close friend and I agreed to accompany her. When I saw that she had booked a pool side room for us, I minded even less, and there was a bunch of other students, including friends of ours, that were also going to ride out the storm at the resort.

At time of check in, the storm was a day and a half out and the weather was amazing. We were sipping rum punch all day pool side and enjoying a steel drum band in the evening with only a slightly higher than normal wind to indicate that anything was different. If not for the Weather Channel showing the monster storm that was now category 4 with sustained winds of 155 mph and the eye wall set to pass in a direct hit over St Kitts, I would have thought I was on vacation.

By about 11 PM of day 2 the winds really started to kick up, the hotel manager ordered the bar closed, the band to clear out, and everyone to their rooms. Heavily buzzed on rum punch, I still had little concern for what was to come, and then the full brunt of the storm came.

The winds were so strong and howling so badly that Nicole and I had to literally yell to hear one another. Huge palm fronds and all manner of debris could be seen flying through the air. Nicole and I were concerned about the sliding glass doors that opened to the pool that a flying projectile could crash through them, so we propped one of the queen mattresses against the doors and slept on the floor on the side of the other bed facing away from the doors.

We did not really sleep as much and we both drifted in and out of sleep with all the noise. Suddenly in the middle of the night, all sound stopped and one could hear a pin drop. I walked outside and opened the doors and there was not even a ruffle of a tree. I turned to Nicole and told her that it was over and we were safe. She reminded me that it was far from over, that we were inside the storm's eye that is remarkably calm.

Within minutes, the winds began to kick up again and the rain started; and seemingly in no time, the storm was not only back in full force, it was worse than the first half; far worse! The night did not seem to end and the noise was deafening. We would later find out that the eastern side of the eye wall had several tornadoes within it shooting gusts of winds in excess of 185 miles per hour.

At day break the brunt of the storm had passed and it was tropical storm like conditions. There was no power and running water and our view from the volcanic mountain on which the resort sat gave us a bird's eye view of the utter devastation of Frigate Bay. The golf course that to this day is the center of the Frigate Bay that services all of the resorts was non-existent - just one big lake in the center of Frigate Bay. St Kitts is shaped like a pork chop with the northern part being the widest. Frigate bay is a thin tapered region of the island, only about ¼ mile across from east to west, Atlantic Ocean to Caribbean Sea. The storm surge came clear across this section of the island temporarily leaving no land distinction between Atlantic and Caribbean other than the sturdy buildings that did not get wiped out.

Once the brunt of the storm had passed we waded in knee deep water to our homes to assess the damage. My friend Bob's condo sea wall had been obliterated and his condo filled with waste deep water. As we grabbed and salvaged what we could we saw fish swimming around his rooms and crabs in his cupboards.

Thank goodness for my friend Nicole's good sense to evacuate to a shelter. Our condo complex was three stories and her condo was on the top floor on the southeast corner. In that region, the roof had been torn off and all of her appliances sucked out the top and thrown out of the condo. Her refrigerator was 75 yards toward the Atlantic Beach as if it had been thrown by Superman. It clearly had been hit by one of the tornadoes within the backside of the storm and she would have surely been killed had she stayed to weather the storm.

The rest of the island was a scene of utter devastation. Outside the tourist district with the island being essentially a third world country, the weak tin roofed structures that the majority of the locals lived in mostly gone, little more than trash heaps left behind in the storm's wake. As much as the students suffered, I cannot even imagine how terrible the situation was for the true islanders living out in the countryside.

Amazingly, my condo which was on the second floor survived having only a few blown out windows and taken in ankle deep water. My roommate and I were able to quickly clean up and our place became a student refugee camp. For the first week following the storm was had 6 students living with us.

It was difficult and hot but circumstances like this with no power and running water really brought out the inner resilience of the students. Every morning, the students living in my condo complex along with our storm refugees would gather in our bathing suits by the pool with buckets to bathe. We would eat canned goods or grill breakfast on our propane grills. We flushed our toilets by pouring 5 gallon buckets of pool water into the towers of our toilets. The pool was overflowing with water with all the rain so there was no shortage of water to bathe with and flush our toilets and we had pre-storm prepared bathtubs full of water to use to brush our teeth.

School amazingly was only closed for 3 days despite nearly ⅓ of the student body being homeless and there was no power or running water anywhere on the island including the school. The school had no generators and the heat in the classrooms was stifling without air conditioning (temperature that time of year was still 98 plus degrees with 100% humidity). I had ink smears on my notes from sweat dripping from my nose onto my writing and I packed three shirts each day of school as each got drenched with sweat in the duration of the day.

Anatomy lab was extra miserable. With no power to keep the cadavers cool the school's solution to keeping our cadavers from rotting was to have the students dip them in a big vat of hyper concentrated formaldehyde a known carcinogen and at these high concentrations, caustic to our sinuses and airways. We were coughing with our noses and lungs stinging, eye watering. To this day I hope and pray that that experience will not have any latent ill health effects.

As proud as I am of my veterinary alma mater, this was a low moment for the school. For an education that ultimately cost me $187,000, I expected better...either be prepared with generators on a known hurricane prone area or at least close school until power was restored and veer off their precious schedule. Such were the sentiments of most students.

Our stoic Dean exhibited zero empathy for the students. Having been approached by the class reps of our Student Government Association about the unsafe and otherwise abysmal conditions the school was subjecting students to (⅓ of whom were still homeless), Dean Dennis one week after school was back in session post hurricane finally came in to speak to each class.

He basically told that the living under such conditions was a test of character and resilience, traits that would ultimately be tested on a daily basis as doctors. In other words, his attitude about all this was, "suck it up buttercup." Nonetheless, per Dean Dennis, the school was taking proactive measures among was sending large permanent generators from the continental U.S. to be concreted in to power the school's walk in refrigerators, computers and air conditioning.. They were to arrive in 2 weeks. Two weeks! Gee, thanks Dean!

Luckily at home in Frigate Bay I was fortunate that the town was a priority because it housed most of the island's major resorts. We got running water back in 5 days. Power was ultimately restored in about 10 days. At the school, power was restored 2 weeks post hurricane, one full week before those wonderful generators arrived.

Possibly the worst aftermath of the storm was the mosquito blooms from all of the pooled water all over the island. One literally had to run to the car in the morning to avoid the swarms of mosquitoes trying to eat us alive.

That flooded golf course I wrote of? That was not to be operational again for another year.

Another interesting aftermath of the hurricane was all of the hurricane romances that followed. Living in tight quarters, bunking with one another, and leaning on one another through trying times, closeness developed between people that were previous not on the romance radar for one another. I was no exception and a relationship developed between my friend Nicole and I.

Like many of the other romances that came out of the hurricane, mine with Nicole was short lived. Within just a few weeks we both realized that we were far more compatible as friends. We not only went back to being friends, we became the best of friends and remained so throughout veterinary school and for years beyond.

Little by little, our homes got repaired and life got back to its routine. Many structures remained damaged for years and some were never rebuilt, but we simply became numb to that reality. 3 more hurricanes would hit St. Kitts, powerful Cat 2 and 3 storms but none with the wrath of George. We were such seasoned storm survivors that the threat of storms began to phase us little as time went on.

Chapter 17 - "...A part of the world and a world of its own all surrounded by the bright blue sea." - *Margaret Wise Brown, The Little Island*

Not much changed on the island other than the weather cooling slightly (from 100 degrees and 100% humidity to high 80's with 80% humidity), not even daylight savings time as the winter approached with St Kitts having never adopted daylight savings time. This was a time when email was just starting to become a common mode of communication but still there was no social media. Calling home cost $3 plus per minute, so we rarely telephoned home. This resulted in students living in our own suspended reality on the island, very cut off from the goings on of the rest of the world.

Case in point, I was wonderfully surprised one semester by my brother, sister, and childhood best friend Steve when they conspired with classmates of mine to fly in clandestinely for my 25th birthday. One of my friends covered my eyes as my family entered the bar at Doo Wop Days Cafe much to my astonishment when my eyes were uncovered.

I had my buzzed short and styled spikey on top and my brother commented that he liked my hair as it was styled like that of Ricky Martin, the pop singer who had taken the U.S. and the world by storm at the time. I asked him who Ricky Martin was and my brother was floored by how out of the loop and cut off from mainstream I was.

When Thanksgiving (a holiday unique to the U.S.) came, my friends and I made a Thanksgiving dinner minus the turkey. With no turkeys on the island, we made a chicken instead but still managed to have stuffing, instant mashed potatoes, apple pie, and most importantly, one another.

Island life felt both magical and unreal at the same time like we were lost in some Bermuda Triangle like vortex almost feeling like we were on the show Lost (that show premiered many years laters but it always reminded me of my life in St Kitts).

When I returned home to NJ for my 2 week winter break following my first semester, my family found me changed, a more laid back and less vociferous version of myself. As I once again experienced the hustle and bustle of NJ, I felt weirdly disconnected from it and simply did not react as I had before. My family found me happy and content, yet more quiet and introspective than they were accustomed to seeing me all of my life. I listened more than I talked whereas before, I was a Chatty Cathy. As much as I was not necessarily looking forward to jumping back into the grind of school and was really enjoying having access to fast food again, in short time I yearned to return to my island. Part of that was perhaps of course because winter is very cold in NJ and in St. Kitts winter is nonexistent.

As my first semester in veterinary school plugged on and finals approached, I was pleasantly surprised that while it took more discipline and work than undergraduate college, veterinary school was really quite manageable academically. I also met the person that would become the second great love of my life, an upperclassman young woman from England named Cara (not to be confused with my classmate Cara from Florida).

Cara was in 5th semester and we had never met. On the last Saturday evening leading up to the grind of finals that students would dare go out, I walked over to my favorite karaoke bar Doo Wop Days for dinner, drinks, and amateur singing. As fate would have it, Cara made a rare appearance there that night with friends. She was strikingly beautiful, blonde with blue eyes the color of a gray sky and adorable freckles on her upper cheeks and nose. I do not remember how it happened, but I ended up sitting near her and when she spoke with her posh English accent I was done for.

I was even more done for when she stood up to sing the Madonna club version of "Don't Cry for Me Argentina." As it turned out, Cara was a classically trained singer and had an amazing, angelic voice. We got along great and never had a pause in conversation that night. I was clear that I very much wanted to see her again when she dropped the bomb that she had a boyfriend. Darn it!

However, there was a caveat. As it turned out, she really did not like the boyfriend anymore, had tried to break up with him before but it caused so much drama, she just figured she would stay with him until he left the island for clinics (he was in 7th semester and set to shortly start clinics at Oklahoma State in a few weeks) and not rock the boat. So, we left it wishing one another well on finals and we would pick it up the next semester when boyfriend would no longer be there.

It was a good plan but we ended up not entirely sticking to the plan. One evening I was at the anatomy lab reviewing my cadaver for the final lab practical coming up. Cara had been walking by the lab and saw me there and came in to bring me food. She thought I may have been hungry and could use a snack since I was going to be there late. How thoughtful! She also suggested that we get together to study at my place to grind away with the absorption of information sharing the same space. You can probably see where this was going.

Our study sessions became a regular thing and in our school on our little island, rumors were very difficult to suppress and people got talking. I caught the boyfriend who heretofore I had never met; giving me the stink eye more than once at the cafeteria but that was as far as it went.

After final exams were finished, many of the students were not flying home for another day or two so the whole school went to a dance club in Basseterre called Mangos and the boyfriend was there. As it turned out, I had learned that he happened to be from NJ as well and many guys from NJ had little qualms about throwing down, and some dude macking your girlfriend was certainly grounds to throw down.

When he saw me, he made a B-line straight for me and told me that he had had it with me hanging around his girlfriend while shoving me (or at least trying to). Having completed my first semester of veterinary school and enamored with his girlfriend, I had no interest or intention to engage in a physical confrontation but I was getting concerned that there may be no other way out of this dilemma. As if on cue, Cara walked through the entrance, saw what was going on, and yelled for me to follow her out the door and I quickly obliged. Her car was parked right in from of the club and we jumped in with boyfriend in pursuit. As he pounded on the window to let him in, Cara lowered it a crack and told him they were through and she never wanted to see him again; and we sped off.

We parked back at the beach and walked, and talked under the moonlight and we both parted feeling as if we were living in the clouds. In two short weeks of knowing one another, we had fallen hard for one another. She was heading back home to her adopted stateside home Virginia the next day and I was heading back to NJ. I gave her my number and asked her to call me at home in NJ when she had a chance.

The very night I after I got home, I was up in my room and my Dad came in wearing a grin on his face. He told me there was a girl with a lovely English accent on the phone. It was of course Cara. Her connection flight in Puerto Rico had gotten cancelled and they put her up in a resort for the night. We spoke and missed one another, both wishing my flight connection had gotten cancelled as well so that I could be in the same resort with her at that moment.

So there I was, back in NJ, happy to see my family and friends, but as I alluded to earlier, feeling disconnected like I did not belong there anymore. My friends noticed the difference in me as well and were shocked to see me pull out a box of my Caribbean brand of cigarette and light up (like many other students, I had unfortunately picked up smoking in veterinary school).

With the red tape still in process in getting her down to the island, Tiffany had not joined me on the island the first semester. When I first saw her, she greeted me as she would have greeted any stranger at the door, wagging her tail and friendly but not with the urgency she had previously greeted me when she was my puppy. I was about to be really sad then within a few seconds, she gave me an extra sniff, looked up, and the recognition flowed back in a rush and she went crazy greeting me, crying with joy at our reunion. We rolled on the floor together for 30 minutes, quite the reunion! She had been sleeping in my Mom's room while I was away but my first night back, Tiffany was snuggled in bed with me like no time had ever elapsed.

That first winter break was fun. Being a veterinary student alone was something unique among my friends and peers but being a veterinary student living on a Caribbean island was just downright interesting and I found myself always the center of peoples curiosity peppering me with questions. My vet school BFF Nicole was from Brooklyn so I was even able to hang out with her one night when she and her friends drove out to NJ to hang out with my hometown friends and I.

The really difficult part was my high school sweetheart Kristen. Although we had not spoken much and I had not seen her for 3 plus months, we were still technically together. We spent time with one another but there was definitely a space that had come between us. Since having last seen Kristen, I had had a brief post hurricane romance with Nicole and was in love with another person. Other than her teaching career, I did not even ask how she had been spending her time since I had left.

Still, despite both of us sensing the inevitable, we did not have the heart to discuss it, as if this break at home was to be our last hurrah. Besides, I had to admit that a part of me really enjoyed spending time with Kristen again. There was so much history between us (by this time we had spent more than ⅓ of our lives together) and few people knew me as well as she did. Weill on my way to fulfilling my dream, she was sincerely very happy for me and proud of me. We parted as friends but really never spoke much again after that.

In recent years, Kristen became a friend on social media and I was so happy to see that she is a happily married mother of three living at the Jersey Shore. We still to this day have mutual friends and by all accounts she remains the wonderful person I always knew her to be.

My vet school classmates and I would ultimately see that many students in committed relationships back home would not withstand their time on the island. This is why when upperclassmen heard that a first year student had a boyfriend or girlfriend back home, both males and females alike would often cynically say, "Not for long." We even saw many marriages fail and later on as upperclassmen ourselves, we would tell the first years the same thing.

Despite my enjoyment at reconnecting with friends and family back home, I was excited to get back to my island and even back to the grind of school to continue my march toward achieving my dream.

I returned to the island two days before school was set to start. Cara had my flight number and time I was coming in and surprised me at the airport and picked me up. We resumed right where we left off only now in the open with no constraints of a boyfriend to keep it from. Semester 2 was off to a great start before school was even in session.

Cara, my friends and I did a bit of partying and enjoyed the beaches in the days leading up to the beginning of school. Like the upperclassman that crashed our welcome reception, many of us crashed the welcome reception for the new incoming 1st semester class. I found it so humorous to see their expressions of excitement mixed with some apprehension. It seemed like an eternity ago that I was an incoming first semester student yet it had only been 4 plus months prior. I wondered if I had worn that same expression at my welcome reception.

Once school started and having a clear understanding of what veterinary school entailed, I was less uneasy about the upcoming semester than I had been when entering 1st semester. Having ultimately finished my first semester with a comfortable 3.4 GPA certainly helped to alleviate any sense that

I may be in over my head. Nonetheless, I was still in the first three semesters, the primary "weed out" semesters that carried by far the highest rate of failure than in later semesters. I was not going to leave anything to chance.

One awesome upgrade to my island experience in semester 2 was having my dog with me on the island. Tiffany just loved the island of St. Kitts with no restrictions about having dogs on the beach. A water dog through and through, Tiffany ran the beach and swam with me just about every day. My best friend and I were reunited and she always helped to keep my spirits up.

Semester 2 proceeded and I quickly got back into my routine only now with a girlfriend I was all too happy to make time for. We were thankfully out of hurricane season and the milder weather and lack of rain in the winter and spring months on St Kitts were delightful.

Another very fun difference in 2nd semester was buying a boat. A 7th semester student was selling his old but sturdy 17 foot center console Boston Whaler and I did not hesitate to jump at the chance. Free weekends were even more fun with the ability to jump on the boat and head over the Nevis, the second smaller island of the nation of St. Kitts and Nevis. Nevis was similar to St Kitts but with a slightly different flavor, in some ways even more laid back with different attractions to see, namely the world famous Four Seasons Resort.

Back then the resort was not very uptight about non-guests enjoying their amazing beachside pool area provided we bought drinks and food. As we visited the resort more often and befriended resort staff (tipping well really helped this cause), we would occasionally even get to make use of the pool side cabanas. It was really nice to enjoy the resort staff making towel pillows for our lounge chairs as if we were guests (that paid between $700-$1500 per night to stay there), come around with trays of finger sized pieces of fruit, and spritz us with Evian spring water as we lounged.

We also expanded our circle of friends with my friend Nicole having begun dating a guy named Mike from our class who we had previously not really known well. He had his own circle of friends that he introduced to us and so helped us extend our social circle. Cara also introduced my group to her upperclassmen friends which made for an interesting social circle that spanned across classes, not common in veterinary school.

After the completion of my second semester, Cara came back to NJ with me to spend the 2 week break with me at my parent's house in NJ. My childhood buddy Brian was getting married in a very ritzy affair at the Four Seasons in Washington DC timed perfectly over my break so I got to introduce my entire network of home town friends to Cara. No surprisingly, Cara charmed the pants off of everyone with her stunning good looks, English accent and bearing, and quick wit. All approved, as did my family.

We returned after the break, Cara about to start her 7th and final semester, me about to start my 3rd. We were as happy as ever but her departure for clinics edged closer and we could not shake the feeling of foreboding as the day approached that she would be assigned her clinical school. She ultimately was assigned LSU, College of Veterinary Medicine.

On the break between 3rd and 4th semester, Cara came home with me once again. My parents had booked tickets for New Year's Eve for a big formal dinner party, as this break coincided with New Year's Eve 1999, the official close out of the millennium. I had also been working with my Mom to help me purchase and engagement ring for Cara, as I was going to propose to her over this break.

Cara and I were really at a place where we endeavored to spend the rest of our lives together, so I felt that if I stepped up with a symbol of that commitment, the reminder of her ring and my knowledge that she wore it while we would be apart; it would help us weather the distance that was to be between us for the next 2 years.

Without hesitation, Cara said yes and we spent the New Year and the next year plus of our lives as fiancés. I felt as if I were on top of the world. Veterinary school was to not only provide me with an amazing career, but also be the place where I found my future wife.

Chapter 18 - "Hard times may have held you down, but they will not last forever. When all is said and done, you will be increased." - *Joel Osteen*

4th semester was rather gloomy for me to say the least. It was my first semester on the island without Cara. As happy as I was that she was at LSU wearing my ring, it did not help much with the void I felt with her absence. I had not done veterinary school without her for two plus semesters.

The subject matter of 4th semester, while a necessary part of our curriculum, was for me very uninspiring. Epidemiology is the study of disease morbidity, mortality, geographic patterns, spread, and containment. Pathology is the study of disease and its effects on the body. Pharmacology is the study of drugs, their mode of action, their metabolism and elimination, toxicity, and indications. Toxicology is the study of toxicity...toxic plants were an especially enthralling part of that course (not sure of the sarcasm is coming through in my words on that one). At least, I thought, there was Avian Medicine. I will learn bird medicine, that's interesting! Boy was I wrong! The course was predominantly the medicine chickens and turkeys as food animals with only less than one month of studying companion bird medicine.

At the same time that the courses of 4th semester were boring me to tears, it was summer again and we endured two hurricanes. They did not nearly match the devastation of Hurricane George in my first semester, but we still lost power for days at a time.

A good friend of mine started not showing up to school and when I next saw him with a severely gaunt frame, I realized why. He had gotten helplessly addicted to crack cocaine, a sadly abundant vice among the locals on the island. There was nothing anyone could say to him that would make him stop. Ultimately, one of his classmates telephoned his parents who flew down to escort him home and put him in rehabilitation. He never again returned to veterinary school.

The icing on the cake of that miserable semester was a girl that had sat next to me in the back of the classrooms for the past 3 plus semesters. We chatted every day but were not especially friends. She never really went out socially but nonetheless I liked her because she was nice and funny. For nearly a week she had not shown up to school. We would shortly thereafter find out that she had committed suicide.

That felt like the last straw to me. I called my Mom in despair telling her that I needed to take a leave of absence and take a semester off, come back with a clear head after I had put all of the negative experiences of 4th semester behind me. Having completed more than half the semester, she convinced me to stay, arguing that it would be foolish to throw away all that work I had already done and delay my graduation, serving only to keep me from Cara longer.

Afterward, Cara surprised me with a plane ticket to go see her at LSU during my mid semester break. Between this and my Mom's pep my resolve to stay the course strengthened and I ultimately stayed. Seeing Cara at LSU really brightened my spirits. She brought me with her to her clinical rotations so I got to see a glimpse of what clinics would be like. She had befriended the student that was in charge of taking care of Mike the Tiger, the LSU Tigers football team mascot. What an incredible experience it was to play with a 300 pound tiger!

Seeing Cara it also felt as if no time had elapsed. Our love for one another was just as strong and every moment we were together, we had just as much fun as always. Cara was laying down plans for our wedding that was to take place once I graduated. She wanted us to marry in her home village in the North of England at a medieval estate, which sounded incredible. Most importantly, while we missed one another dearly, the distance was not seemingly making a dent.

I returned back to the island reinvigorated and ready to finish 4th semester and put it behind me. 5th semester loomed with courses that held the promise of feeling very doctor-like with courses like Small Animal Medicine and Anesthesiology. I was beginning to see the light at the end of the tunnel.

Chapter 19 -" ...let me congratulate you on the choice of calling which offers a combination of intellectual and moral interests found in no other profession." - *Sir William Olser*

5th semester did indeed make me start to feel like I was transforming into a doctor. All of the semesters prior simply lay down the foundational information - a mountain of information - that would serve as the basis of medicine and surgery. In the simplest of terms, medicine and surgery are collectively applied anatomy and physiology.

In 6th semester, we began surgery lab, radiology (the reading of images as in x-ray, CT scan, MRI, and ultrasound) and delved into equine (horse) medicine. We constantly performed physical examinations to establish clearly defined normal findings and vitals so that later on in clinics and as practicing veterinarians abnormal findings would be clearly evident. We constantly combed through diagnostic laboratory data to provide a strong foundation of clinical diagnostics.

By my final 7th semester, in addition to completing our final course work, we would divide our time between the classroom in the morning, and rotating through the school's teaching hospital in the afternoons. This included medicine, surgery, emergency and clinical care (complete with overnight on call duty), ambulatory medicine (farm call medicine), and radiology. It was a very exciting time to find ourselves putting all of our learned disciplines together and being molded into veterinarians, while getting ready to move on to our clinical years, the final leg of a long road.

Cara was much further along, interviewing for jobs in NY on the verge of finishing up her clinical year at LSU and graduate. Ross University graduation back then was at Lincoln Center in NYC and Cara's walking ceremony occurred during my break between 6th and 7th semester. This was convenient since Cara was able to stay at my parent's house and Cara's mother was able to come to her graduation and stay with my parents as well. Career-wise, these were exciting times for both of us.

Personally, unfortunately, our busy lives full of transition and planning for two very different realities (her preparing to start her first employment as a veterinarian, me preparing to start clinics and pass national board examinations), our relationship was not the same. Being so preoccupied, we spoke less, travelled to see one another less, and in some ways had become strangers to one another.   Still, we stayed together and stayed the course with our engagement with the hope with the end of our transition and in the near future being settled in our careers, we could focus on us again.

In the middle of my 7th semester, the administration asked us to submit our top 3 choices for us to attend clinics in order of preference. With Cara in mind primarily, knowing that she was going to take a job in in NYC, my top two choices were Cornell and NC State given their proximity to NY only a drive or quick, short flight away. My third choice was University of Illinois primarily because I had friends that had gone on to clinics there that reported back great experiences.

The decisions as to where students were sent for clinics had really little to do with merit and more to do with the university wanting to send students to each school that would accurately represent the overall student body. At the time, the school found that the best way to do this would be to average out the GPA's of the incoming students to a given clinical school. They accomplished this by matching A's with C's and a few B's added in. In this manner, the clinical schools would respectively receive a group of our strongest students, weakest students and several in between.

As my luck would have it, I ultimately got my third choice, University of Illinois. I was not disappointed at all knowing that I was headed to complete my clinical training at a fine school with Ross students that I had alluded to earlier that had given me excellent reviews on their experience there.

Knowing that I was coasting through 7th semester will little to no threat of failing, I began the process of preparing to leave the island for good. My brother had come down to visit me early in 7th semester (throughout my tenure in St. Kitts, he would ultimately visit me once each semester), so I sent my dog Tiffany back with him where she would await me at my parent's house.

I then sold my car, microscope, and several textbooks to incoming first years, and started shipping non-essentials back to the US. I sold my boat to a local Kittitian that I had become good friends with who intended to use the boat to run snorkeling and dive tours for tourists. I spent my final month on the island with little more than bare essentials that would ultimately fit in two suitcases.

I ultimately breezed through final exams and I knew that this time when I boarded my flight back to the US, I would not see my little island for a long time. I said my goodbyes to my friends that I had known for only 2 years, 4 months of my life but I felt as if I had known them all of my life. All of that time in class together, in labs together, studying together socializing together, and weathering hurricanes together formed a bond between us that to this day is unique and unyielding. There were a lot of tears of joy and excitement considering that, like the 7th semester student who spoke to us at our 1st semester orientation, we too had made it.

When I returned back to NJ, Cara had been living in my childhood bedroom. This worked out conveniently given the easy train ride from the neighboring town that she could take into NYC for her interviews. By this time, she had taken a job at a small animal clinic on the Upper East Side and was set to move in to her new apartment. My family and I helped her with the move when I was home on break between finishing up at Ross and reporting to clinics at Illinois. We parted and I went back to my parent's house to prepare for my journey to Illinois.

Thankfully, I had not sold my Explorer and I returned back from the island to a vehicle. My Mom had used it occasionally to keep the tires from dry rotting and mechanisms from seizing and it was in good shape and ready for the 13 hour drive to Champaign-Urbana, Illinois.

By the time of my trip, I had already reserved an 800 square foot studio apartment in the middle of campus to rent for the year. I had my driving directions printed out from MapQuest ready to go. GPS was still not yet standard in cars or smartphones. In fact, very few people in 2001 had smartphones and I was no exception, thrilled to be back from the island and sporting a flip phone again. Tiffany and I climbed into my SUV and headed out for our long drive across the Appalachians followed by the flat plains of the Rust Belt.

As I headed west, I saw the number on my exterior temperature gauge consistently dropping. I figured it was because of the elevations of the mountains, but as I got to Ohio where the land was as flat as a pancake, the temperature kept dropping.

I found the landscape as I entered Indiana rather depressing and monotonous. The land remained flat, the highway straight as an arrow, and there were endless stretches of muddy cornfields having I been plowed months before. Although it was day time and there were no clouds, the sky still seemed constantly grey.

Illinois was no different as I entered the state. Surprisingly, even within 30 miles of the school there was still no change in scenery. Having just lived on a tropical island for the past 2 ½ years, this most certainly was a big change. It was not until just a few miles from campus that I started to see more homes, stores, gas stations and signs of civilization.

Between taking breaks, stopping for gas, and walking Tiffany, I arrived to campus at about Noon. It looked like a typical college campus with students out and about, dormitories, fraternity houses, and lots of bars. I stopped at the rental agency, picked up my keys, and headed to my new place.

I chose my domicile for the next year well. It was located on Green Street, right in the heart of campus where all of the most happening restaurants and bars were, plenty of shopping walking distance, and several open dog friendly quads to exercise Tiffany. The apartment itself was small but completely renovated with new fixtures, countertops, and appliances. The toughest adjustment was the weather. From the moment I had arrived, the temperature had not risen above 17 degrees and according to the forecast that was not to change any time soon. My time on the island had most certainly warmed my blood.

It would be two days after I arrived until I started my new rotations so I used the time to stock up, get my phone and cable turned on, and learn my way around campus. I took a dry run to campus to time it during rush hour so that I would leave myself ample time to arrive early and avoid being late on my first day.

My first day of clinics was orientation during which the incoming Ross students were given a tour of the teaching hospital, handed our rotation schedule, and given a brief tutorial on how to use the teaching hospital computer software to enter our medical notes, charting, entering laboratory requisitions, and entering department consultation requests.

Our guide was the Chief of Internal Medicine, Dr. Thomas Burke. Dr. Burke congratulated us and told us how much he and the faculty enjoyed taking Ross students with our admirable preparation, knowledge base and work ethic. He told us in the 4 years Illinois had been accepting Ross students they had never had a bad one. He repeated "never had a bad one," as if to warn us not to be the first.

We were dismissed around 3pm and were each to start our respective rotations the next day. We were naturally each a bit nervous about starting rotations. The Illinois senior class we were about to join had been in clinics since May 2000, so in January 2001, we would be joining them more than halfway through their clinical year making them seasoned veterans and us complete newbies fresh off the island.

I would have liked to have had dinner and a few drinks with my classmates but, while my Ross classmates that accompanied me to Illinois were nice people, they were not particular friends of mine that I had socialized with on the island. So instead, I went home and made myself homemade lasagna and enjoyed a few glasses of wine while hanging out with my dog back at my apartment. That was sufficient to calm my nerves and I turned in early.

My first rotation was anesthesia. As I was instructed, I was to enter the anesthesia treatment suite and join into rounds. The group of students I was to join just stared at me as I walked in with my scrubs and white coat on and stethoscope around my neck. I broke the ice my saying, "Hi everyone, I am one of the new incoming Ross students. My first rotation is Anesthesia. Am I in the right place?" They all quickly relaxed and promptly introduced themselves. The reason for the tenseness was that they thought I might have been a new intern or resident.

From then on, the Illinois students on my first rotation could not have been nicer, going out of their way help me learn protocols, show me where the injectable medications, syringes, catheters, and bandaging materials were kept. They even invited me out to join them at The High Dive that Saturday, a popular campus club.

Although I was inspired to one day be "The Man In The White Coat," ironically, I could not stand wearing the white lab coat that many doctors wear and was required attire for all clinical students at Illinois. I found them bulky and stifling and preferred to just wear my stethoscope around my neck in just my scrubs on procedure days and shirt, tie, and khakis on receiving days. I would occasionally get reprimanded by a clinician for not wearing my coat, but within a few months they pretty much gave up and my white coat hung in my closet never having gotten broken in. It remains to this day stiff as a board.

Anesthesia was a fun rotation starting each morning claiming our cases, performing physical examinations, and tailoring the premedication, fluid therapy, and anesthesia protocols of each patient based on lab data, the procedure it would be undergoing, and physical examination findings. The procedures the patients would go through ranged from surgeries to dental cleanings, CT scans or MRI's, and even radiation therapy.

One evening during my on call week during the anesthesia rotation, I got called in at midnight, along with my supervising senior anesthesiology resident, Dr. Lamonte. The case was a dachshund that had gone acutely paralyzed in the rear limbs due to a disc rupture in its back. The patient was to undergo a decompression surgery but the exact location of the disc herniation had to be determined with a CT scan. Dr. Lamonte assured me that the most tedious part would be the CT scan but once in surgery, things would go rapidly since the senior surgical resident that was called in to perform the surgery, Dr. John Silbernagel, was known for his precise but speedy efficiency in surgery.

Once the diagnosis was confirmed by the radiology resident that read the CT scan, up we went to surgery and in walked Dr. Silbernagel. I was 26 at the time and I judged that Dr. Silbernagel could not be more than 3-4 years older than me. Despite his youth, Dr. Silbernagel took charge of the operating room and the surgery with quiet confidence that exuded his self-assuredness, yet did not cross the line of arrogance.

As Dr. Lamonte had promised, Dr. Silbernagel breezed through the surgery. Although my primary responsibility as the anesthesia student on the case monitoring the patient's vitals, I stole peeks at the surgery as often as I could. To date, I had performed surgeries in surgery lab under the guidance of our professors, as well as in the teaching hospital at Ross University. I already knew that surgery was by far my greatest special interest, however, upon seeing Dr. Silbernagel in action, I decided that that moment that I wanted to specialize in surgery and seek a residency post-graduation. That sentiment was rammed home further when I learned that within 48 hours of surgery, the dachshund that Dr. Silbernagel operated on was walking.

The second highlight of anesthesia rotation had nothing to do with veterinary medicine. I was on a case that needed a type of x-ray called a myelogram, where x-rays are taken after the injection of a contrast agent into the spinal canal. Because several rounds of x-rays were being taken, I monitored my patient remotely via telemetry outside of the x-ray suite to avoid being exposed to radiation. As such, I was seated next to the x-ray technician control tower where the technicians would set the x-ray technique and shoot the x-rays.

The young radiology technician on this case was a stunningly beautiful young woman, among the most stunning I had ever seen in my life. In between the reading of my patient's vitals I simply could not take my eyes off of her. I heard her fellow technicians calling her "Moe" (rhymes with go). Interesting name I mused.

That night, I went home to check my rotation schedule and I learned that I would not have radiology rotation (during which students worked alongside technicians to learn x-ray positioning and technique) until May. It was only January! Anyway, although things were continuing to deteriorate between us, I was still engaged to Cara.

The sad reality by this time was that my engagement to Cara was falling apart. We could hardly talk on the phone without getting persnickety with one another. As a result, we talked less and less.

She flew out for a brief visit during my next rotation, internal medicine, which did not go well. I thought that she had changed a great deal since our dreamy days on the island; she thought that I had changed as well. We mutually agreed to break up just a couple of weeks after she returned from her visit and shortly thereafter, returned her engagement ring to my Mom over lunch in the city.

I was both very upset but on some level relieved at the same time. That last thing I needed in the middle of my clinical year while also studying to pass my national board examination was relationship drama. Nonetheless, it was hard to not think about the time we spent together in a whirlwind romance that spanned two countries and had taken us both by storm. In the coming days, I would leave many tears on Tiffany's shoulder. My beloved dog was a master unconditional consoler. She would be the only individual to see how emotionally hurt I felt.

Chapter 20 - "Coming out of your comfort zone is tough in the beginning, chaotic in the middle, and awesome in the end...because in the end, it shows you a whole new world." – *Manoj Arora*

Even after having expanded my cultural horizons in St. Kitts, arriving in Illinois was still a bit of a culture shock to me. Although I was in the microcosm of a major university, farm culture dominated every aspect of life.

Many of my newly adopted classmates grew up on farms and when not in the hospital wore cowboy boots, Wrangler jeans, and flannel shirts. Country music blared everywhere. Our early spring social was a hoedown.

Some of my more humorous experiences during my clinical year (at least from the perspective of my fellow students and supervising clinicians) was during my farm and large animal rotations. Much of it resulted from lack of significant exposure to farms and farm animals.

On my first day of large animal livestock rotation, I saw a llama in one of the runs. His name was Duke and I learned that he was actually a permanent resident of the school having been donated. Duke lived a life of comfort with access to the best health care, while students got to learn from working with and caring for Duke. Apparently in the Midwest, llamas are very popular pets.

Llamas are really funny looking animals and I could not wait to get up close to Duke. Very accustomed to people, he walked right up to me but once he got close, he reared up and spit a wad of thick saliva that covered my face. Dr. Hadad, the senior supervising resident, burst out laughing. She informed me that llamas are commonly weary of strangers and are prone to spitting at people that they have never met that approach them too boldly. She then kindly let me excuse myself to go to the bathroom and wash my face.

During equine rotation, we made a farm call out to breeding facility where we were to artificially inseminate several horses. After each student completed his or her task, we were free to walk around the grounds.

I came upon a paddock that had a few horses in it and I called out to them. A really friendly one trotted right up to me but would not come any closer than within 3 feet of the wire fence so I could not reach to pet him. No matter how much I coaxed him, he would not come any closer.

I decided that I would approach him and as I grabbed the wire fence to reach over to pet the horse, I felt a jolt of electricity that knocked me to the ground. The clinician in charge of me, Dr. Shipley, may have been a board certified theriogenologist (reproductive specialist) and a PHD, but he was very much a farm boy. He ran out of the barn (apparently I had yelped when I got shocked) and found me sprawled on the ground still dazed trying to figure out what the heck had just happened to me.

When I told my clinician what happened, he asked me, "Why hell did you grab an electric fence you dumbass?" When I told him I did not know that it was electrified, he replied, "You don't recognize an electric fence?" I replied, "No, where I am from, we only see electric fences surrounding prisons." To this he said, "Dam city boy," and walked off.

Unfortunately for me, aside from getting spit in the face by the llama and electrocuted by an electric fence, I was otherwise quite good at large animal medicine and my clinicians took notice. One day, my ambulatory medicine clinician needed volunteers to pull blood from 400 head of cattle at the crack of dawn at an Amish farm to check the herd for an infectious disease called Brucellosis. Although I did not raise my hand, Dr. Miller picked me anyway despite other students still having their hands up clearly itching to go. When Dr. Miller read the confusion on my face, he smiled and said, "Sorry Roger, you may be a city boy, but when it comes to proficiency at bleeding cattle, you are like a savant. It will go much quicker with you there."

Also unfortunately for me, I was quite good at pregnancy checking dairy cattle. For those of you unfamiliar with how one pregnancy checks a cow, it involves covering your entire arm with a plastic sleeve, making a fist, and shoving your entire arm up the cow's rectum to feel the uterus below it.

One day, Dr. Miller had a farm call where 70 head of cattle needed pregnancy checking. Guess who got volunteered even though I was not raising my hand to go?

While I did not particularly care for large animal medicine, it was a very good experience for me overall. I learned a great deal about the farm industry and how meat and milk make their way from farm to store to table and the economics of farms in general. .

I learned that pigsties are so loud that working inside them without ear plugs could permanently damage your hearing. After one week of working in a pigsty treating pigs, I had the smell of pig (not pleasant!) on me for two days no matter how much I bathed. I learned that for pig farmers working within their sty every day of the lives, the smell never comes off.

I got to work with $100,000 horses and people who were the level of crazy that one would expect of a ones that would pay $100,000 for a horse. Most of them came in already sure of what ailed the horse, just simply needed the veterinarians and hospital to implement the treatments....they were never right of course. I also learned that whatever goes wrong with the health of a horse usually occurs at 2 AM.

I got the opportunity to get out of the hospital and work outdoors and most importantly, learned that I had the ability to excel at something that was well outside my comfort zone

Chapter 21 -"Our third love is said to be the one we do not see coming...the third love is the kind that comes too easy and doesn't seem possible." - *Nadia Makarova*

May rolled around and I was about to start radiology rotation when it occurred to me that at last I would work with the beautiful technician named Moe. To my dismay, when the techs gave us our orientation, Moe was nowhere to be found. I did not see her the rest of the day so I assumed she either changed jobs or maybe I was mistaken and she was actually a student, intern or resident (although I could have sworn that she was wearing the navy blue polo that constituted the University of Illinois veterinary technician uniform).

Assuming that I would not ever meet the beauty named Moe, I reported to the radiology technician station the next day after rounds and walked in on Moe sticking her fingers in fart putty and faking the action of blowing farts. This, of course, served to make her even more attractive to me.

I learned that Moe was not there the day before because she had taken the day off for her birthday. The fart putty was one of her birthday gifts from her fellow technicians. When I worked my first case with Moe, I asked her about her unusual name and she explained to me that her name was actually Melissa. Her coworkers called her Moe because when she got hired there was already a Melinda working in radiology they called Mel as a nickname and they felt it would be too confusing to have two Mels; hence the birth of Moe. From then on, however, I called her Melissa and she did not seem to mind.

She had blonde hair with blue eyes that had a hint of hazel near the pupil and a perfect figure....like I said, stunning! But what made her all the more attractive was the quiet confidence with which she worked, by far the youngest tech on that service at 22 years old, but clearly carrying the respect of all her fellow radiology techs, including the head tech, Sam.

I was clearly smitten and although my fellow students and other technicians noticed that I went out of my way to get on cases with her and flirted with Melissa constantly, she seemed oblivious to my efforts. I thought that she may have been too professional to date students, was simply not interested, or some of both. With a complete lack of any sort of hint of interest from her, very uncharacteristically for me, I had a very hard time to summon up the confidence to ask Melissa out.

On my second week of radiology rotation, after we finished our cases for the day, I followed her out into the parking lot at a distance to see which car was hers. The next day at lunch time, I left a note on her windshield with my cell number letting her know that a bunch of students and I were going to Buffalo Wild Wings on Saturday for drinks and karaoke and I would like for her to join us. She called later on that evening and said she would meet me there with her friend Kerry who was an oncology technician.

Melissa and Kerry showed after I had arrived and we chatted over drinks, played some darts, and Melissa got to hear me sing Billy Joel's "It' Still Rock n' Roll To Me." She was drinking a sparkling wine called Raspberry Framboise that came in a fancy glass that she commented how much she liked. She and Kerry suggested that we go to another bar that they liked and when they hit the restroom prior to leaving, I grabbed Melissa's empty Framboise glass and shoved it down my pants. I walked her to her car and before she got in, I handed her the glass in my first act of chivalry (or petty theft, depending on the perspective).

When we entered the next bar, there was a upper and lower level. The upper level had a railing you could lean against to look down into the lower level that was a dance floor. There was country music playing and there were lines of people doing what looked to me like marching in unison. Remember when I eluded to the culture shock I experienced in Illinois?

I asked Melissa what the people on the dance floor were doing. With a perplexed look, she turned to me and asked, "You've never seen line dancing before?" I told her that I had never heard of it and changed the subject.

Melissa was clearly in her element in this country bar with country music and line dancing. It was not particularly my taste but I couldn't care less, I was finally hanging out with Moe. We talked with ease and as we approached the end of the night when I went to ask her out on a one on one date, what came out was, "Would you like to go out and grab a burger some time?" What?? What was wrong with me? I was never this awkward around females! Thankfully, she said yes and the next weekend we went out to dinner at Chili's and went to see the movie Pearl Harbor and had a great time.

The second half of radiology rotation was interesting because I had to finish my rotation while having a budding romance with Melissa. She of course was very professional but I just could not help myself. This was a time before digital x-ray was standard, so we had to develop our x-ray films in a dark room. I repeatedly tried to lure her into the dark room to make out, but like the good girl that she was, she resisted.

After radiology was over, I was pleased that I had gotten an A on the rotation. The doctors' grading on our ability to interpret the images represented 75% of my grade, while the technicians' grading of our ability to position and take x-rays collectively represented 25% of our grade. Melissa was the only technician (or doctor for that matter) to assign me a B! I asked her what the deal was and she steadfastly stated that I received the grade that I deserved. This of course, made me yet more attracted to her!

The more I got know Melissa, the more she impressed me. She came from very humble means in a tiny farm town called Hinckley, Illinois with a population of less than 800 people. Her graduating high school class had 60 students and her high school combined the students of 3 towns!

She attended one of the best veterinary technician programs in the country called Parkland College of Veterinary Technology. She was able to get out of her small town because of her own achievement, having gained admission to a very competitive school and even earned grants to help pay her tuition. While in school, she worked at a barbecue place called Long Horn Smoke House and she continued to work there part time in addition to her University of Illinois job to help her to save for her future while getting a jump on paying down student loans.

Part of the reason Melissa continued to work the second job was because her boyfriend prior to me had managed to steal money from her bank account to fund a cocaine habit she knew nothing about until she found out the money was missing.

The ex-boyfriend actually came from successful and loving parents that put him in rehab once they found out what was going on. Very decent people, they offered to let Melissa live with them until she could get back on her feet after their son had stolen all of her savings.

At the teaching hospital, I would use any excuse I could get to head down to radiology to I could see Melissa. If my rotation ever had a patient that needed x-rays, I would be the first to volunteer put in the requisition and take the patient down there. Most students avoided radiology like the plague because there was always a big line for x-rays and the head technician Sam was a stickler for first come, first serve with the exception of unstable or critical patients.

On one occasion, I was on cardiology rotation and patient was due for a heart ultrasound, but the resident in charge realized that the referring veterinarian had never taken chest x-rays, a crucial first step in a cardiac work up. He was dreading how much this was going to back up his day with this one case knowing the traffic jam that seemed to always persist in radiology. I told the resident that I may be able to help get the x-rays sooner if I could excuse myself and walk down to radiology. He told me to go ahead and good luck performing whatever miracle would get me past the formidable Sam.

I was able to get Melissa's attention between her cases and asked her if she could finagle some priority for the cardiology case and told her how good it would make me look if I could pull this off. Melissa herself was a stickler for the rules, but to my astonishment, she told me she would do it and to go and get my patient ASAP; and to not tell a soul what she was doing for me.

I ran back to cardiology and told them that I would be taking the dog down immediately for chest x-rays. When I returned, the resident and students were all looking at me with smirks on their faces wondering what connection I had in radiology to get radiographs go quickly. I told them that unfortunately, I was sworn to secrecy.

Secrets, however, are not easily kept in a veterinary teaching hospital and my resident, Dr. Prozek, found out the next day. When I walked into morning rounds he said, "Moe? Really? How did a little punk like you land that little cutie?" Dr. Prozek was a very cool resident.

Although it was a little strange that every night I kissed Melissa good night she was going home to her ex-boyfriend's parents' house, Melissa and I became very close, very quickly. Despite having just recently met, being with her was just natural. We did not really go out that often, having a blast just going to the Laundromat together to wash our clothes, cooking dinner in my studio apartment, or doing one of our favorite things to do together: rollerblading.

Only 6 months away from graduation, I had not planned on it, but I was in love again.

Melissa Eastabrooks 2001

Chapter 22 - "Power is neither good nor evil. It just is. It's what people do with power that matters." - *C.J. Redwine, The Traitor Prince*

By in large, my veterinary education brought me the opportunity to learn under incredibly talented and inspiring professors, clinicians, residents, and even interns. In my clinical year, however, I learned that there are a bottom dwelling minority of people that readily use their position in charge of others to be abusive rather than inspirational, and behave more like dictators and less like leaders.

In the veterinary teaching hospital, the hierarchy is clinicians at the top, followed by residents (of which there are junior, senior, and chief residents), interns, and then students. As I alluded to earlier, early in my clinical year, I was immediately inspired by a gifted young senior surgery resident, Dr. Silbernagel, who provided me final confirmation that I was determined to seek out a surgery residency to become a surgical specialist.

This was my thought process as I entered my soft tissue surgery rotation. My fellow students and I on rotation were under the supervision of senior resident, Dr. Michael Singer, first year junior resident, Dr. Shawn Kennedy, and intern, Dr. Brenda Salinardi.

I cannot for the life of me recall what I may have done to offend Dr. Kennedy, but it was clear that he did not like me from the outset of my rotation. He was always quick to pounce on my answers in rounds, would interrupt me as I presented my cases in rounds, and always was eager to pepper my presentations with gotcha questions and catch me off guard. On the latter, he was largely unsuccessful in catching me unprepared. While one would think that a dedicated educator may be pleased with his student' preparation, in Shawn Kennedy's case, it seemed to instead frustrate him.

During one week of the rotation, the local pound brought in several dogs for students to spay and neuter to get students practical surgery experience while providing the shelter with free sterilizations, a win-win for both school and shelter. Unbeknownst to me, my first patient that was to be spayed was in early estrus, commonly referred to as being in heat. She was too early to be showing outward signs of estrus but far enough along that her uterus, ovaries, and associated blood vessels were all enlarged and dilated internally.

This type of circumstance creates a lot more bleeding and requires a larger incision since the organs of reproduction along with their blood supply are significantly larger. Thus, in the course of this surgery I had to contend with constant bleeding that I needed to control which contributed to a more labor intensive procedure. Having performed abundant surgery on the island while attending Ross University, I was not frazzled, perfectly in control, and well prepared for this curve ball.

To save surgical time, as I was tying off bleeders and major vessels, I occasionally grabbed the suture needle with my fingers to pass through and tie my knots. In surgery we technically are instructed to avoid this whenever possible and focus on grabbing suture needles primarily with our instruments. That stated, in the real world, surgeons commonly grab needles with their fingers whether the circumstances require it to pull a suture needle around a fragile structure without damaging it or if it would simply save time.

As I was ligating one of the ovarian arteries, Dr. Kennedy came over and said, "Welton, do not grab the needle." To this I stated "Yes sir, just trying to save time because this patient is in heat and has near constant bleeders." His reply to me was, "Complications are not aided by being careless."

As I was finishing the ligation of the uterine body, the final step of the hysterectomy, the enlarged uterus presented me challenges in getting adequate exposure to get my ligation suture around the pertinent anatomy. Ever cognizant of Dr. Kennedy's reprimand, I passed the end of the suture underneath the uterine body that did not have a needle attached but grabbed the needle when I tied my knot so as not to risk the pointy object dragging across end piercing any organs or vital structures.

Despite several of the University of Illinois students moving painstakingly slow through their spays (without the benefit I had of so much hands on surgical experience at Ross, this was a first time solo surgery for every one of them), Dr. Kennedy kept laser focus on my procedure and saw me grab a suture needle again. This time he stated, "Welton, I told you not to touch the needle." To this I clearly recall replying that I had good reason to do in under this circumstance order to avoid pricking vital vasculature with the needle. He refrained from commenting at all on my reason and said, "Touch the needle one more time and you are scrubbing out."

I was raging inside at this would be Napoleon when I caught the eye of the intern who gave me a sympathetic look. She fully understood what an ass Kennedy was being but being his subordinate, the intern, Dr. Salinardi, had to watch her back as well. Still, I appreciated her empathy and closed my surgery without further incident or comment from Dr. Napoleon.

The next day I had an uncomplicated spay. With lack of complication, I finished the procedure in under 30 minutes while, again, my Illinois student colleagues took much longer (it took one student nearly 2 hours to complete her spay). I was finished too quickly for Dr. Napoleon (after the "grab your needle" incident this became my private name for him) who came over to nitpick, and as the technician was removing the drapes, Dr. Napoleon said, "Done pretty quickly Welton." To this I said, "Yes, this is spay number 9 for me so it is becoming pretty routine for me." To this he replied, "Routine or careless, we'll see if she lives."

Dr. Napoleon did not know that I had already decided to adopt this dog before I spayed her and I answered, "Not only is she going to live, she will heal faster and less painfully with the benefit of my minimal incision and spend her life with a DVM who loves her." When he looked perplexed, the technician filled him in that I was taking the dog I named Lulu home with me.

Shortly after, Dr. Napoleon had his own solo surgery, the first of his residency. When interns, residents or surgeons had solo surgeries, the students would gather around and watch. It was a very simple abdominal exploratory surgery with a few biopsies of the intestines. Dr. Napoleon took his first biopsy, just a small wedge of tissue and when he went to close it, passed his suture what did he do? He grabbed the suture needle with his fingers!

I could not resist and in front of his supervising senior resident and all of the students on rotation (who were all privy to our strained relationship), "Hey Kennedy, touch the needle one more time and you are scrubbing out." The senior resident, Dr. Singer, let out a small laugh and all of the students had to suppress their grins, but Dr. Napoleon glared at me with fire in his eyes. He replied, "How much longer are you on this rotation Welton?"

"One week."

"I'll be glad to be rid of you."

"That makes two us."

Despite being the most competent student surgeon in my rotation, I would later learn that Dr. Napoleon gave me a D for the rotation all for personal reasons. Granted, I did not need to egg him on at the end the way I did, but his constant dishing out of abuse was inappropriate. And while I have always possessed the ability to accept well-meaning constructive criticism, I have no tolerance for abuse.

Luckily the senior resident, whose grade carries more weight than the junior resident, assigned me an A, as did the intern, leaving me with a net A for soft tissue surgery rotation. Still, it really stuck in my craw that a so called professional in such an important institute of higher learning would go out of his way to try to devastate my career, not because of any lack of proficiency, but simply because he did not like me. Dr. Napoleon knew that I wanted to be a board certified surgeon and had he succeeded in assigning me a poor grade on surgery rotation for mere petty and personal reasons, there would be very little chance of that ever happening.

While Dr. Napoleon and I thought we were done with one another, the rotation schedule had other ideas and placed us together yet again for orthopedic surgery rotation. By this time, I had spent a month of off block (students get 6 weeks to have rotations of our choice off campus at other accredited veterinary hospitals) at the prestigious Animal Medical Center (AMC) on the Upper East Side of New York City on a preceptorship in none other than orthopedic surgery. What's more, down an intern that had to leave abruptly for a family emergency, the surgical service at AMC treated me and essentially utilized me as an unofficial intern.

I had an incredible experience at AMC and left hoping that I would match there for a residency. I had worked with their Chief of Surgery, Dr. Parker, quite a bit, as well as several of their staff surgeons and gained a great rapport with them. There were no Dr. Napoleon types and that further encouraged my interest in residency at AMC.

On my first day of orthopedic surgery now back at Illinois, while I was less than thrilled to see Dr. Napoleon, I was pretty excited to work under senior resident, Dr. John Haburjak. I had heard great things about Dr. Haburjak as a surgeon, a young resident that sincerely enjoyed teaching students, and being a generally personable and funny guy.

Dr. Haburjak and I clicked right away. Fresh off the AMC orthopedic surgery rotation, there was not a question that I did not know the answer to in rounds and our personalities meshed. The best part was that Dr. Napoleon knew that his supervising resident and I had a great working relationship and subsequently for the most part, he left me alone.

On one occasion, however, Dr. Napoleon could not help himself to try to take a dig at me. I had used a suture pattern for a closure that I had learned at AMC to close deeper tissues. In rounds the next day, Dr. Napoleon questioned why I had chosen that particular pattern since it was not appropriate given the circumstances. My answer was blunt and truthful, "I learned it from Dr. Parker, Chief of Surgery at AMC in that exact same situation; figured he was a pretty solid example to follow and the result was great." Dr. Napoleon had nothing to say to that and I could see Dr. Haburjak grinning.

Another pivotal moment that would profoundly affect the direction of my veterinary career occurred on this very rotation. Before I explain, it is first important to provide a bit of background to the story. Dr. Haburjak did not hide the fact that he did not particularly care for the Chief of Surgery at University of Illinois, Dr. Anne Johnson. Dr. Johnson was a rather accomplished surgeon, particularly in the field of orthopedic surgery, so respected that she wrote the orthopedic section of the most widely used small animal surgery textbook in veterinary academia. Dr. Johnson, unfortunately, was also known to be a bit of a hard ass, a "my way or the highway" type of educator and leader.

Dr. Haburjak pre-residency had spent 5 years in general practice, making him a seasoned veterinarian in the "real world" well before applying to match for a surgery residency. He was confident, highly capable, and possessed the free spirit of a California native. He most certainly did not appreciate authoritarian type personalities.

During one particular particularly troubling time in the teaching hospital, there had been cases of an outbreak of a bacterial infection with a strain called listeria that had emanated strictly from the surgery department. The outbreak was ultimately traced back to contaminated IV fluid bags and the entire batch was discarded.

Not satisfied by the discovery of the contamination, Dr. Johnson ordered that all surgeons, residents, interns and students had to wear bouffant surgical hats when in the operating room, banning the more traditional surgical caps many wear. Generally, the bouffant caps were used by women (and some men) that had long hair, as the hair net type style of the cap made it easier to cover long hair. Most men wore the more traditional caps that tie in the back and in many of our opinion, kept shorter hair back more effectively (not to mention, looked less silly).

Many of us had fun with surgical caps, ordering custom made caps. Raised a NY Yankee fan, I had a NY Yankees camp that I wore with pride in a teaching hospital where most people were Cubs or White Sox fans and generally hated the Yankees. Dr. Haburjak had California motif surgical caps with waves, surfboard, palm trees and such.

I was a bit disappointed that I could not wear my Yankees cap especially since it appeared that surgical caps had nothing to do with the listeria contamination. Still, best to pick one's battles and I decided not to defy the ever powerful Dr. Johnson over a fashion statement.

However, on the first surgery that I was to serve as Dr. Haburjak's assistant, he showed up in one of his regular custom caps, not in a bouffant. I asked him if he'd heard about Dr. Johnson's order and he answered, "Yes, but I don't care because I am morally against following stupid rules." His answer made me like him even more.

The surgery was quite complex, a Cocker Spaniel that had fractured both of the major long bones that comprised the elbow joint, the ulna and the humerus. Dr. Haburjak told me to make sure I had eaten and used the restroom before surgery, as we would be in surgery for for 2-3 hours.

Just prior to surgery as we were scrubbing, Dr. Johnson came in to check on Dr. Haburjak to offer her two cents and make some suggestions about the surgical approach, vital anatomy in the area, and certain plates and screws that she would recommend. Dr. Haburjak curtly but politely enough nodded and said thank you. Knowing his body language at this point, I could tell that Dr. Johnson generally irked him.

During the course of the surgery, once the most technical work was completed and we were closing, Dr. Haburjak asked me what my goals as a veterinarian were. I told him that I wanted to match for a surgical residency just as he had done. His response shocked me when he replied, "Don't."

Dr. Haburjak went on to explain that at this point he was months away from his residency completion, but if he had known what a residency would be like, he would not have done it. His exact words as he elaborated why were, "Roger, you remind me a lot of me and I will tell you that I have struggled with eating shit and saying yummy from the likes of people like Anne Johnson for the past three years. On top of that, your compensation for taking abuse and breaking your back performing surgeries that bring in multiple thousands of dollars a year for the school is a poverty level $20,000 per year stipend."

He went on to enlighten me about the legalities and logistics of veterinary medicine where a motivated and talented doctor can venture into any specialty they like without the necessity of formal residency training. Dr. Haburjak suggested that I choose a practice to work for that was staffed with experienced doctors

142

already skilled in specialty procedures and diagnostics that would train me, while actually earning a real, livable wage right out of the gate. He also noted that for any surgeries that my future mentors may not necessarily have expertise in, several surgical equipment and hardware corporations offered advanced postdoctoral surgical training for general practitioners to gain expertise in highly technical procedures.

This gave me a great deal to think about the direction of my future. I understood everything he was saying and he had opened my eyes to a reality that I was not fully privy to; that I could still be a highly skilled surgeon without the necessity of prolonging my life in academia for 3-4 more years. By this point loving my life with Melissa and actually entertaining the idea of proposing to her, starting the first fews years of marriage earning a poverty wage also did not seem an attractive idea to me.

Still, I was torn on how to proceed with the clock ticking on my window to either start putting out resumes seeking employment in general practice or apply to match for a residency. A run in with another abusive intern on equine (horse) rotation would make the final decision for me.

Equine rotations at any veterinary teaching hospital are notoriously busy. Students could be juggling 4-5 cases at once while still having to work emergency and ICU overnight shifts. Overnight emergencies are hit or miss in small animal, but are a virtual guarantee on equine since horses tend to get seriously ill in the middle of the night, most commonly a gastrointestinal emergency called colic.

One night, another student and I took in and managed 4 colic emergencies while still having to treat the 7 horses in the ICU ward. Two of those cases were mine that I was to present their vitals and progress at rounds at 7 AM. One of my colic cases ended up having to go to surgery and I had to stay with the patient until I passed it along to the surgery service and an equine surgery student took over my case. By this time it was almost 6:45 AM and I had not yet had the opportunity to examine and write up one of my two cases for rounds (although all of her treatments had been completed).

Having worked all night non-stop, exhausted and bleary-eyed, I presented my cases in rounds and explained that my emergency that got referred for surgery took me right up nearly to rounds and I would update vitals and examination findings as soon as rounds were over.

An intern, Dr. Aimie Doyle suddenly spoke up and accosted me saying, "This is unacceptable, emergencies are no excuse for not having been fully prepared to present your case in rounds. You need to manage your time better." In no mood to take abuse from an intern I replied, "Dr. Doyle, short of cloning myself, I am open to suggestions on how I could have stayed with a critical patient and examined and written up my perfectly stable medicine cases to present for rounds." After my response the resident in charge, Dr. Thomas, stepped in and told me to just get it done right after rounds and present to her one on one.

I thought this was the end of it since I had no further incidents with Dr. Doyle and we interacted completely normally. As the one month rotation went on, however, fellow students started telling me rumors that I was going to fail equine rotation.

I had no idea what they were talking about. With the exception of the one morning when I had the emergency that delayed my presentation for rounds, I diligently kept up with my caseload and every one of my patients not only recovered, but the clients were happy with my care and communication. What's more, the teaching hospital protocol was that if a student was in jeopardy of failing a rotation, the supervising doctor (typically a senior resident or clinician), the student was to be alerted and a meeting set up with the Dean of Students so that the student was made aware of why his/her performance was below grade level and the steps he/she needed to take to raise the grade.

Here I was with one week left from completing my one month equine rotation with no such notification that I was in danger of failing anything, yet according to half the people I knew, I was going to fail. Luckily, my friend Lydia who was on an equine fast track (she wanted to be an equine veterinarian) filled me in on what was going on.

Knowing that our resident Dr. Thomas was heavily boggled down with cases and relying a great deal on Dr. Doyle to manage the students, Dr. Doyle was going to submit a failing grade for me, meanwhile advise Dr. Thomas that I deserved a failing grade based on attitude and performance. She assumed that Dr. Thomas would go with her recommendation having been too distracted to assess otherwise.

I approached the Dean Students about this and rather vociferously let him know how appalling it was that an intern would take one confrontation, never again address it, then not only scheme to smear my career record as a personal vendetta, but gossip to my student peers about it.

The Dean assured me that failing to have followed protocol, no clinician in this circumstance would be permitted to submit a failing grade. What's more, Dr. Doyle would not be permitted to have any say in my grade for this equine rotation, I was not to work any cases she was in charge of for the remainder of my equine rotation, and she would receive a documented reprimand for unethically discussing a student's performance with other students.

All had turned out in my favor, but at this point I decided unequivocally that I was done with the academic pecking order. I would never allow petty and abusive people to have influence over my life ever again. I was going to take Dr. Haburjak's advice, complete my clinical year, and join a cutting edge general practice.

Chapter 23 - "At last there is a light at the end of the tunnel." - *Joseph Alsop*

I had taken my Clinical Competency Test in Springfield, Illinois in June 2001 and passed with flying colors. That is the national board examination that is necessary to pass in order to legally practice veterinary medicine in the United States. In late July with more than half of my clinical rotations under my belt, a clear understanding of the kind of veterinary career I wanted, I headed home for the first two weeks of the total of four weeks the university allotted clinical students for off block. I took the opportunity to fly back to NJ to start interviewing potential jobs and get some Jersey Shore time in with my high school and college peeps.

Seeing all of my friends was a wonderful treat as always. One particular buddy of mine, Dave, was (and still is) a great guy and friend, but not really the sentimental type, had some very kind words for me. He said, "Hey Roj, I can't believe you are almost done. As long as I have known you, you always wanted to be a veterinarian and here you are so close to that dream. Do you know how few people in this world ever follow through to achieve a childhood dream? Unbelievable man, I am proud of you."

In the midst of working through one rotation to the next, studying for boards, and courting Melissa, what I was on the verge of accomplishing had really not yet set in. Hearing Dave's words really put it into perspective for me and partying with my old friends "down the shore" as we say in Jersey, never felt so sweet.

My interviews were very interesting. At the time with 5 associate veterinarian jobs available for every single veterinary graduate, I felt as if it was more like I was interviewing the employers, not the other way around. After 5 interviews, I had narrowed down my choices to two practices in the beautiful Long Island North Shore town of Huntington, NY.

One practice was a 3 doctor practice with the fourth having been recently forced to retire early due to health reasons called Fort Hill Animal Hospital. If I took the job, would be his replacement. The hospital dated its founding back to 1895 and was an old Victorian mansion that was converted into an animal hospital. The owner, Dr. Henry Travis (called Hank by all of the staff) was a very friendly, informal, and laid back man who was known for his exceptional skill in the operating room.

The other practice was an enormous, glamorous facility with big pillars in the front with architecture, decor, and equipment where clearly no expense had been spared. West Hills Animal Hospital was a 9 doctor practice and I would be their tenth if I took the job. The owner, Dr. Alan Coren was very friendly and one could tell, very sure of himself. To his credit, I think to this day, I have not seen a privately owned practice as impressive in scope as West Hills Animal Hospital. Dr. Coren offered me $5000 more per year in salary than Fort Hill did.

While money was important with student loan bills set to start rolling in 6 months after graduation, it was not at the top of my list as far as my first job was concerned. I wanted first and foremost, a high end animal hospital accredited by the American Animal Hospital Association (AAHA). Accreditation by AAHA is voluntary and involves a rigorous inspection process and medical records audit to prove that cleanliness, equipment maintenance, record keeping, and medicine and surgery meet a veterinary university standard. In short, when a clinic becomes

AAHA accredited, it is announcing to the world that they do it right.

Secondly, I wanted solid mentorship progress in my surgical and medical skills but without being micromanaged. Both of these owners and practices offered these criteria.

Ultimately, the deciding factor was the warmth that I felt from Hank. Dr. Coren was nice enough, but I could see a level of deference in the manner in which his employees treated him and everyone called him Dr. Coren; whereas the whole staff called Dr. Travis "Hank." I decided that I would work for Hank.

Renewed after a 2 week visit home to spend time with friends and family and with my first job secured, I headed back to Illinois to continue my March toward graduation. I had some interesting clinical rotations to look forward to and of course, I dearly missed Melissa who kindly apartment sat for me and baby sat Tiffany and my new adoptee, Lulu, while I was away.

I felt as if I was in coasting mode at this point. Having passed boards, secured employment, and with graduation in my sights, I had endeavored to keep my head low, refrain from anymore confrontations even with abusive supervisors, and finish out my year without incident. At this point, nothing was worth jeopardizing so much that was just within my grasp, even if it took playing the role of academic sheep that so many students and subordinate doctors did out of fear. A bit of hurt pride was a small price to pay for a lifetime of freedom from such compromise.

In early September, 2001, I had another 2 week off block. By this time, Melissa and I were inseparable. She had taken me home to meet her parents and siblings in the sleepy farm town of Hinckley, Illinois, and all had gone well.

With graduation looming, I had had the conversation with Melissa telling her how much I loved her and wanted to make a life with her; and floated the idea of her moving out to NY with me. To my elation, Melissa was excited about the idea of it, but she would have to finish out her apartment lease to fulfill her obligation to her roommate prior to moving (her lease was up in June, 2002 so we would be apart for only 6 months during which time we intended to fly to visit one another).

In light of this, I asked her to come home to NJ with me for the upcoming off block in early September. It would coincide with Labor Day Weekend at the Jersey Shore with the weather still warm and the parties off the hook. I reserved us a bed and breakfast for Labor Day Weekend on the beach in the town of Sea Girt.

When we arrived in NJ, my Mom and Dad were very happy to meet my young, Midwest beauty who was as humble and personable as any person could be. My Mom found her simply "adorable." Born the same year (1979), Melissa and my sister Leslie hit it off really well.

Like most occasions when people visited us from out of town for the first time, the Weltons decided to give Melissa the standard tour - a drive out to the Staten Island ferry to Battery Park in Manhattan to walk around the financial district, see the Statue of Liberty up close, and tour the World Trade Center. The date was September 4, 2001.

As we exited the ferry, while the traffic in NY is never light, it was extra stifling for a midday weekday. The sidewalks were swelled with people and there was gridlock. My father - we would come to learn prophetically - at the sight of this mass of humanity said, "Man, I would hate to see what a state of emergency or crisis would look like in this town. What would they do with all these people trapped on the island?"

Eventually, we managed to park, walk around, see the sites, and have a nice lunch near Battery Park. Rather than take the ferry back, we opted instead to jump on the Holland Tunnel to get back to Jersey. Melissa to her credit, was not overwhelmed by the hustle and bustle of the city and generally enjoyed the experience. This was pretty impressive for a girl whose entire town had a population smaller than the number of people at any given one city block in Manhattan.

We flew back to Illinois Sunday, September 9 and I started equine surgery rotation on Monday, thankfully without the intern Dr. Aimie Doyle on service. On the morning of Tuesday, September 11, 2001, exactly one week from the date of our site seeing tour in NYC, as I was driving to school for rounds, the news of the Twin Towers having been hit by planes was all over the radio.

I felt like I was listening to some fake Orson Welles War of the Worlds radio broadcast, shocked in disbelief that this happened. As I got to school, rounds were chaos, as nobody could focus on the job at hand; especially those of us from that area. All I could think about was my college roommate, Mike, who was like a brother to me and at the time working on the New York Stock Exchange whose work frequently brought him into the Trade Center buildings. I tried calling him and all communications were down. I could not even call my family in NJ across the Hudson.

To his credit, the Dean of Students made an announcement that all students with family in the greater NYC area were excused from rotations and invited to the faculty lounge to watch the live news coverage. Another student and I (both of her parents were financial analysts in the NYC financial district and she was distraught) entered the lounge just in time to see the reporting that the first tower had collapsed. The second tower collapsed about an hour later. I began to despair that I may have lost my friend and countless others I knew that worked at the Trade Center.

Watching the news was doing me no good, so I instead went to the computer station near equine surgery and see if Mike or anyone else I was worried about had emailed me information. There was none.

Melissa found me at the computer station, worried herself, as she had met Mike on our recent visit back to NJ. She liked him very much and she knew how close we were. She put her hand on my shoulder not knowing what to say and I stood up and hugged her. That steadied me more than any words could have. I even went back to my rotation and let my supervising equine surgeon know that I was collected and ready to work. I felt the best thing I could do was immerse myself into cases and keep my mind occupied on anything but Mike's status.

Later on, I had dinner at Melissa's condo and I got a call from Mike. He was back in NJ and safe! After the second plane hit, Mike had the foresight to know not only was this clearly a terrorist attack, but that all exits out of the city would soon be shut down. He was able to get on the last ferry out of Battery Park, not only safe, but having avoided getting stranded as many thousands did in the aftermath of the attack.

Everyone who was alive during the 9/11 attack will forever remember exactly where they were at and exactly what they were doing the moment they first learned of the tragedy. As I write this, I can picture like it happened just yesterday, sitting at a stop light, looking on at the University of Illinois dairy farm, listening to the radio in disbelief as I listened to the events unfolding.

Chapter 24 - "Unless commitment is made, there are only promises and hopes; but no plan." - *Peter F. Drucker*

My gratitude for Melissa and the faith that she put into our relationship moved me deeply. Here was a young woman who had recently been terribly betrayed by a man and had just managed to put her life back together; now willing to move with a person she had only known for 4 months, to a place that was as foreign to her as another country. She did not consider the consequences of things not working out and as far as she showed me, that possibility did not occur to her.

I did not want to take this for granted and intended to honor Melissa's faith in us with a real tangible commitment from me - I planned to propose to her before year's end.

I began my scheming by calling my Mom who had the engagement ring that I have previously given to Cara. The ring was beautiful, 1.6 carrots sitting on a platinum band. I told her my intention to ask Melisa to marry me and she told me that she and my Dad fully approved. She then said that she would take the ring to her jeweler to have the diamond swapped out for its equivalent, since apparently it is bad luck to re-gift a diamond from a failed engagement.

I then called her parents to ask their permission to ask their daughter to marry me. I will never forget what here Mom said to me, "I could not have hand picked a better son in law for my daughter." That was amazing!

The next part of my plan was to have Melissa fly out for a week over the New Year for a ski vacation in the Pocono Mountains in Pennsylvania. Having been born and raised in pancake flat Illinois, Melissa had never skied before so I thought this would be a fun, new experience for her. I was going to present her the ring at the top of the mountain when we got off the lift. I was set to finish my last clinical rotation, ophthalmology, in mid-December and I would be home for good by then.

The rest of my year finished up uneventfully and I packed up and prepared to leave Illinois for good. Knowing I was going to see Melissa in just a couple of weeks after arriving home, saying goodbye was not sad at all. We both saw our parting as temporary and were looking forward to our future together (even though she did not know I had a ring for her).

I made the long drive back with my two dogs and settled back into my old childhood bedroom. Between transferring of transcripts, national board exam results, and state of NY Office of Professions processing time, I would not be fully licensed to practice until late January, 2002, giving me a tentative start date of February 1 and roughly 6 weeks to find a place to live in Huntington, NY. Naturally, finding my apartment was my first priority.

While out home hunting in Huntington, I stopped into the practice to see Hank and he gave me another quick tour, introduced me to techs and other employees that I had not previously met, and showed me my office. He briefed me that his plan for me would be to shadow him for 2 weeks then ease into cases seeing appointment once every 30 minutes (as opposed to more experienced veterinarians that see appointments every 15 minutes) for the first month.

My biggest challenge was not finding a suitable apartment, but finding a landlord that would allow me to have my dogs. Melissa also had a Yorkie or her own and a cat but I did not mention her pets so as not to push my luck.

Amazingly, I found the perfect place the first day I was looking. It was one bedroom, one bathroom apartment that was the upstairs of a two family house. The landlord would allow my dogs provided I placed an additional month's rent, non-refundable pet deposit. The current tenant was to move out at the end of December; giving me all of January to paint and make the place our own (all with Melissa's input, of course).

Melissa flew into Newark Airport on December 27. She had already met my family so she was quite comfortable. My Mom even let her sleep in my bedroom knowing that I was about to pop the question.

Patience has never really been a strong suit of mine and this time was no different. I was juiced with excitement about proposing to Melissa, but I also had this paranoid feeling that I would misplace or lose her ring if I carried it around for too long. So....I proposed to her that first night when we were alone in my bedroom. She said yes!

The next morning when we all came down for breakfast, I told everyone and all offered their sincere congratulations and welcomed her to the family. My Mom told me that she knew that I would not be able to wait until we were in the mountains. My Mom knows me well.

Nonetheless, we had an amazing ski vacation. Never having skied before, Melissa took her lumps on her first day, but she sucked it up and kept at it despite sporting some pretty nasty bruises on her hips. By day two she was really getting it and by day three, a day my brother and cousin, both seasoned skiers who had driven out to skin with us for the day, were amazed that this was the first few times Melissa had ever skied.

In the evenings, we enjoyed nice dinners, hot tub, and wine by the fire in our cabin. It was a magical time and a great way to mark the beginning of our lives together.

We parted after that vacation as fiancés. Our target wedding date was to be some time in 2003 with the main planning phases to begin after she had moved out and settled with me in NY. While we would miss each other, Melissa was set to move out in May and we were not very sad. I was also already planning to fly out to see her in later January and her to fly out to NY again in March to interview for jobs and help give our new place her female touch.

I felt that I was living on a cloud, a licensed veterinarian with my dream girl to spend my life with and our whole lives ahead of us. Every morning I awoke, I had to remind myself that all of the blessings were really occurring and I was not dreaming.

Chapter 25 - "Far and away the best that life has to offer is the chance to work hard at work worth doing." - *Theodore Roosevelt*

Without Melissa around to help me set up the apartment, my awesome Mom came out to Huntington help me paint, buff and finished the wood floors. Melissa had picked out the colors already and had helped me pick out our furniture that was delivered for us. We were to wait on next visit for Melissa to pick out the blinds and curtains.

I moved in with my dogs one week before I was to start my job to give myself the opportunity to join a gym and learn the lay of the land. At this point in my life I had become quite comfortable with moving and adjusting to new places, as well as doing so alone.

I discovered that there was a mountain bike trail called the Green Belt Trail that connected the North and South Shores of Long Island and I could pick up one of its trail heads only a couple of miles from my home.

I also learned that one of the best surf spots in Long Island was in an area called Democrat Point, only a 20 minute drive south of me at Robert Moses State Park. Having loved skiing so much, Melissa was open to also trying surfing. I was already planning on buying her a mountain bike for her birthday coming up in May so we were poised to have a great deal of activities to enjoy together in our free time, Culturally, NYC was only a 40 minute train ride away and locally there were great restaurants, shopping and great estates to tour.

Historically, the North Shore of Long Island was known was The Gold Coast, as it was home to vast estates owned by superwealthy families like the Roosevelt's, Vanderbilt's, and Rockefellers to name a few. As the era of property taxes set in, even these families of immense wealth could not support the immense cost of maintaining such vast estates and many were donated by the great families to the state to be turned into museums and state parks for the enjoyment of the public.

The North Shore was truly a beautiful place with so much to do and enjoy, perfect for two young people just starting their lives to enjoy together. The architecture was a mix of Cape Cod and Victorian style homes and ivy covered stone mansions among the very wealthy areas which were plentiful. As one ventured further east, the architecture and vibe took on more of a coastal New England type atmosphere reminiscent of Block Island, Nantucket, and Martha's Vineyard.

My clinic of employment was situated on a road that hugs the entirety of the North Shore called Route 25A, only a ½ mile from Huntington Harbor and the Long Island Sound. The clientele were generally well off, some crazily wealthy and even included some celebrities. Celebrity clients included:

Pat LaFontaine (Team USA Hockey and NY Islanders star)

Freeman McNeil (former NY Jets star running back)

Billy Joel & wife at the time Christie Brinkley

Dee Snider (lead singer of 80's hair band Twisted Sister)

Perhaps the most wealthy and powerful family we worked with was the Dolans. They owned the Comcast Cable network, the NY Knicks, and the NY Mets.. During my time at Fort Hill Animal Hospital, I became the go to veterinarian for the Dolans, however, I never actually met the Dolans in person. Their

Russian born caretaker would bring the family dogs to the clinic in a limousine. They sent the whole staff free Met's tickets to a game every year which was a very nice gesture although unfortunately, most of us were Yankees fans.

At any rate, the main point I am making here is that I started out practice in a bit of a veterinary fantasy world where cost was rarely a barrier to the best standard of care. Before embarking on a diagnostic and treatment protocol for a patient, we are mandated to first present a treatment plan which itemizes all aspects of care to provide an estimate of cost. Very often, the clients of Fort Hill Animal Hospital would tell me to not bother with the estimate and to just go ahead and get to doing whatever needed to be done.

Hank's plan to have me shadow him only lasted 2 days. On day three, the hospital was slammed with emergencies so Hank had the front desk open me up and said, "Sorry kid, you're going live today." This was actually fine with me...as much as I liked Hank and was picking up helpful tips in how he dealt with clients and patients, in only 2 days, I was already getting quite bored.

Thus, I jumped right in with rarely routine stuff. Since the other doctors were already established with their own clientele and having much of their book filled with their existing clients for routine well care, I saw the entire overflow which consisted mostly of sick and injured pets. This was also fine with me, since I really enjoyed the challenge and fast pace of emergency medicine and surgery.

In addition to Hank, there was Dr. Kenneth Gant (who we all called Kenny) and Dr. Melinda Grove. Melinda had graduated from Ross one year before I did although I did not know her on the island. She was a good doctor but not much more

162

experienced than I was so I relied primarily on Hank and Kenny when I needed advice which they offered graciously.

I always say that I was a young veterinarian born of two veterinary fathers. In Hank, I had the more empirical, hardened experience perspective from a veterinarian who had graduated Cornell in 1974 (the year I was born). Hank practiced good medicine and was an excellent surgeon but as he freely admitted, still retained a lot of his 1974 approaches to cases and medicine. As a 2002 graduate, I obviously did not agree with some of his approaches.

Kenny, on the other hand, had graduated from Cornell in 1993. He had done both his undergraduate and veterinary school at Cornell and in his first year out of school did a one year internship at University of Tennessee before joining Fort Hill Animal Hospital for whom he had worked for the past 8 years. With his impressive experience and youth relative to Hank, I found Kenny to be very current and the consummate academic in in his approach to working up cases.

I was fortunate to have both of these gentlemen, as I took some aspects from each of them as I formed my own brand of veterinary medicine and gained my own clientele that bought into it over time. I also found myself breaking away from them altogether. In one glaring example of this, I did not particularly care for the procedure they used to repair ACL tears of the canine knee. They used a procedure called the DeAngeles technique that was a more dated variation of the procedure I had learned in school. After Hank gave me push back on getting the equipment necessary to repair knees that I wanted to, I ordered the equipment myself.

Feeling that I had defied him in purchasing my own equipment to perform the surgery my way, Hank was at first unhappy with me. He later relented and recognized that it was reasonable for me to perform a surgery in the manner that I am most comfortable. He even had the bookkeeper cut me a reimbursement check for the cost of the equipment.

This was the beauty of Hank. He was there to offer assistance to me and advice; in fact, it was clear that he really enjoyed mentoring. On the other hand, he did not try to micromanage me and gave me free reign for practice my brand of veterinary medicine. Quite oppositely, it seemed that Hank took pride in the independence of his young new associate and my desire to be my own man.

On one occasion he had left his exam room door open a crack and I overheard the conversation he was having with his client being right next door in pharmacy calculating some drug doses. The client was joking about how surprised she was that I was old enough to be a doctor. Hank replied, "Yeah, he looks like he's barely out of high school, but don't let his youth deceive you. That kid is one hell of a doctor and knows his shit."

One thing Hank and I had in common was our love of the NY Yankees. Every morning before the start of appointments we would chat about the Yankees as we sipped our coffee. Beyond the Yankees, he frequently asked me how things were with my fiancé, how I was adjusting to life on the North Shore, and how I liked my career at Fort Hill. In short, Hank was a good man and I felt privileged to work for such a man.

The staff reflected Hanks easy going manner and were very pleasant to work with. I may have been young and new, the low man on the totem pole, yet they carried out my patient orders without question and with full diligence. It did not hurt that my directives always included the words "please" and "thank you." I remembered how much I disliked clinicians in school that barked out orders as if veterinary technicians were their slaves and I had always vowed that I would never behave like that.

There was one young receptionist named Nicole who was about my age that I clicked with. We chatted all the time and she made it her personal responsibility to keep my schedule organized and manageable and kept me on task with my medical notes and timely call backs to clients. The other staff members eventually dubbed Nicole "Roger's secretary."

I still did not really know anybody socially in Huntington so Nicole became my first real friend there. Knowing that we worked well together, Hank put Nicole as the receptionist for my one evening of the week on Tuesday nights. After work we would frequently go to a bar called the Artful Dodger for drinks and meet up with some of the people she grew up with in the area. It was nice to be building a social life again. .

March came in no time at all and Melissa was on a plane to fly to see me in Long Island and see her new apartment. I was elated to see her. Even though I had just been out to Illinois to visit her in late January before I started my job, it felt like ages since I'd seen her in person.

My schedule was pretty cool because although I had to work every Saturday, I had every Monday off. I had to be on call for one weekend per month (including Sunday) but the pay back for that was to get the entirety of the next weekend off. Since my weekday off was Monday, that gave me a 3 day weekend once per month and it was during one of those that Melissa chose to come visit.

It was surreal to have her in the apartment knowing that in just 2 ½ months, this would be a permanent arrangement. We shopped for things for the apartment and Melissa put her personal touches on the place. Melissa is quite the nester and has a gift for making spaces very homey.

When I had to go back to work on Tuesday, Melissa did several job interviews. The way the laws are in NY, licensed veterinary technicians (LVT's) are in high demand. On the job training for technician duties is illegal in NY and a person who is not licensed it not permitted to even administer an injection. As such, Melissa had a lot of offers.

The job she settled on was actually a friendly competitor of Fort Hill, also located on 25A in the nearby town of Northport; called Northport Animal Clinic. The clinic was a family legacy practice under the ownership of the Fredericks family for three generations. The primary owner at the time was Dr. Russell Fredericks who had inherited the practice from his father, Dr. Richard Fredericks (who had inherited the practice from his father). Dr. Richard , aka, Dick Fredericks still practiced part time and maintained partnership in the practice.

The Fredericks family owned a family horse farm in Northport that housed a herd of polo ponies. The family was heavily involved in the local fox hunt club. Besides being a nice, well run practice, one of the big attractions to working for the Fredericks family was the opportunity for Melissa to ride the polo ponies. Melissa's biggest passion in life was (and still is) horses. The ponies needed work and she loved to ride, so it was a win-win for the Fredericks family and for Melissa. The

Fredericks also knew they were hiring a dynamite, university trained technician.

With her future employment secured, Melissa headed back to Illinois. She left quite a void in our little home when she left, but I knew that I would be flying out to Illinois in mid-May to help move her out and take the drive back with her to NY for good.

When the time came, her friends at the U of I teaching hospital threw her a going away party and showered her with cards and gifts. I could tell that she felt some sadness at leaving the job and the people she loved, leaving the state that was the only home she ever knew. Having seen a glimpse of her future, seeing that Long Island was a lot of fun, and knowing that we would be planning our wedding soon, Melissa also was excited. One of the best attributes of Melissa was her sense of adventure and willingness to try new things.

Our first year in NY was amazing. With a dual income, reasonable rent expense, and my student loans not kicking in until the end of August, summer was especially fun. We went to the beach all the time and Melissa learned to surf. We visited the Hamptons, Montauk Point, and took the Montauk ferry to Block Island to spend a few days there.

Melissa and Nicole got along great and between Nicole, a couple of young techs at Fort Hill that we befriended, and a young tech that Melissa befriended at Northport, we had a cool little circle of friends. Our favorite place to go to watch Yankee games and enjoy happy hour was a prototypical North Shore pub called Meehans.

Now settled in NY, Melissa and I started planning our wedding. We were in a bit of a quandary. Melissa's mother was one of nine siblings which makes for an enormous extended family of uncles, aunts, and cousins; most of which would not have had the financial means to fly to NY for a wedding. Most of my immediate family would have likely made the trip for a wedding, but much of my network of high school and college friends would not likely make a trip for a wedding in Nowhere's-ville, Illinois. Our solution was to go off alone and get married and honeymoon in Maui, then have separate wedding parties later on in Illinois and NY and our parents would come to both.

Melissa found an agency online call MarryMeMaui that specializes in arranging private wedding excursions. We arranged a non-denominational Christian wedding on the gazebo of a beautiful resort in the town of Lahaina, with a Hawaiian Christian pastor dressed in traditional ancient Hawaiian cultural dress. He even blew through a conch shell after he pronounced us man and wife and I kissed the bride.

The whole event was professionally videoed and photographed with a beautiful album and DVD created. We spent the following two weeks surfing every morning, taking snorkeling tours, driving the famous Road to Hana, and enjoying an amazing 2 weeks as newlyweds.

After returning and married and our lease was coming up for renewal, Melissa and I were feeling quite settled in NY and were starting to feel the itch to own our own house. My parents were very graciously willing to front us the money for the down payment so we started looking for a modest home to purchase. We ended up finding the perfect 3 bedroom home just a few miles from our jobs and moved in early 2003.

Our lives seemed set and we were happy but there were challenges to come that would dramatically affect the course of our lives.

Chapter 26 - "I found that the standard of living does not go up with the cost of living." - *Warren Buffett*

As most are aware, the cost of living in Long Island, NY is very high and this was the case in the early 2000's when I was living there. Between student loans, high taxes, and paying our bills, Melissa and I found ourselves with precious little income to afford dinners out and even the most modest of vacations. We also were not saving any money for our future.

To address this, I reached out to other clinics to take on extra hours as a fill in doctor, what is termed in the industry as "per diem" employment paid either on a production or hourly basis or some combination of both.

My first hit turned out to be the largest emergency and critical care veterinary hospital in Central Long Island called Animal Emergency Services. Since I was accustomed to seeing overflow emergencies as the newest doctor at Fort Hill, I felt comfortable taking this on and they hired me for Monday nights.

At first, they paired me with a very experienced emergency and critical care doctor name Dr. Matthew Kearns who would turn out to be perhaps the most skilled all around doctor I ever worked with. Matt was extremely friendly and accommodating, giving me my space to work through my emergency cases but freely mentored me in procedures I lacked experience in such as placing chest tubes, using the defibrillator, and certain emergency procedures.

For many of the complex surgeries that needed stat surgery, it was not uncommon for Matt and I to be in surgery together in the middle of the night. It was absolutely exhilarating and the experience I was gaining greatly complemented the experience I was gaining in general practice.

As exhilarating as it was, however, my schedule was quite grueling. I would go into the emergency clinic Monday at 5 PM and work until 8 AM Tuesday morning. By the time I drove home battling morning rush hour traffic it was usually close to or after 9 AM and I would hop into bed and sleep until 1:30 PM, having to the get to my regular Fort Hill evening shift that started at 2 PM until 8 PM (usually not getting out until close to 9).

On top of that, on my one weekend off, I would often fill in at other general practices when asked because living in NY and paying my student loans, it felt like I could not earn enough money to get ahead. As much as I loved my work, veterinary medicine is most certainly not just playing with animals all day. There are sometimes angry owners, aggressive pets, crotchety co-workers and cases that do not go well despite the veterinarian's best efforts. In short, it is not all shits and giggles and some time away from it is necessary to maintain the passion and mentally recuperate, otherwise risking burn out.

In the midst of this, two major developments were occurring with my family and with me professionally. My brother had accepted a regional vice president position with is company that required him to move to Central Florida to an area called the Space Coast because it is the area surrounding the NASA base of operations at Cape Canaveral. My sister took a position working for him and was planning to move there as well, and when my parents went down to visit, close to retirement, they thought that the Space Coast would be a lovely place to retire. This would leave me as the only member of my immediate family remaining in the northeast.

As much as I would have missed them being a drive away, this did not upset me that much. I figured it would be a great opportunity to visit my family on frequent Florida vacations but I would remain in the NY/NJ area where I had grown up and still wanted to live; high cost of living notwithstanding. Quite coincidentally, Melissa's older brother John who she was very close with had moved to Fort Pierce, FL, about a 90 minute drive south of the Space Coast 3 years prior to follow his own career opportunity.

On the professional front, three of the practices that I was doing per diem fill in work for were offering me partnership opportunities (Hank had a daughter that was applying to veterinary school so it was made clear out of the gate that there would be no offering of partnership at Fort Hill). Working crazy amounts of hours just to make ends meet, I understood that practice ownership was my best way to gain a better balance of career and leisure time balance. This was very attractive to me.

On the other hand, accepting a partnership would forever tie Melissa and I to NY and we were not quite sure if this was necessarily our final destination. Although we never really spoke of moving to Florida, I think it was the back of our minds that perhaps it may not be a bad move. Outside of going skiing occasionally winter did not really appeal to us, as we were both very outdoors oriented people.

In February of 2004, Melissa and I decided to take a week vacation to the Space Coast to see my family and drive down to Fort Pierce and visit Melissa's brother as well. We flew out of JFK airport early in the morning in the middle of near blizzard conditions. We landed in Orlando to 80 degree weather and by that afternoon, Melissa and I were on my brother's boat with my parents sipping Coronas.

At one point, Melissa and I turned to one another and said in stereo, "Do you think we should move here?" Clearly we were mentally on the same page. Right then and there, we decided we were moving to Florida.

When we returned from our trip, we put our house on the market and I thanked the clinic owners for the offer to bring me in as partner but politely declined. I did not yet share it with Hank because I did not know how long it would take to sell my house, get licensed to practice in Florida, and gain employment in Florida.

The other big question I had was how I was going to work as a veterinarian in Florida. As I stated, I was increasingly interested in being a practice owner. Partnership is not something that is offered right away but is offered after years of working for a practice and proving that all parties are a good fit for one another.

I had really enjoyed working for Hank but there were many ways in which I would have advised him to run his practice differently. For example, more recent graduates were big proponents of the tenant: "techs do the teching and the doctors do the doctoring." This refers to the fact that technician duties such as taking x-rays, drawing blood, administering treatments, running diagnostics, etc., should be relegated to technicians.

Doctors are not above performing these tasks, but it is poor use of their time and compromises the caseload a doctor can take on when they have to stop between appointments to do these things. A doctor's time is much more productively spent performing examinations, surgery, procedures, interpreting diagnostics and lab data, and making treatment recommendations. Having insufficient technical staff to prevent doctors from having to perform these duties is a bad business model, as it interrupts efficiency and reduces individual doctor production capabilities.

Despite Kenny and I having repetitively advised Hank that the effective metric to promote maximum efficiency in a practice is 2 technicians per doctor, Hank repeatedly dismissed us insisting on one tech per doctor with one floating tech to split among 3-4 doctors on service at any given time was perfectly adequate. The work up traffic jam got so bad at times that the other doctors and I would find ourselves constantly having to interrupt our case flow to perform technician duties for our patients.

This is one example of many areas where I knew Hank could have improved the patient and client care of the practice, increasing the revenue of the practice, and having less frustrated doctors. I did not want to sign up with another practice in Florida where I would once again have to follow the directives of another owner that may not align with my own.

As I thought it through, my decision was simple. As I was going through the process of getting ready to live and get licensed to practice in Florida, I was actively seeking an existing practice to buy in the general area that I planned to live.

I was preferably seeking a one doctor practice for two reasons. First, as a young veterinarian moving to a new state with a limited credit history, I knew that there were limitations on the amount of money a bank would be willing to lend me to purchase a clinic. Single doctor practices were and are generally more affordable.

Second, with a single doctor practice, I could come in and raise the scope of veterinary services and client care to grow it into something worth far more than my initial investment. In my per diem travels working freelance in various practices in Long Island, I learned that one doctor practices were quite limited in the services they provided. Consumed with micromanaging the human resources, scheduling, tax planning and every other aspect of business administration, they had little time or compunction to participate in advanced continuing education to expand their skill sets to perform more advanced and technical procedures.

As a result, they often referred out many cases that were beyond routine. This not only created a mundane existence for the practitioner, but it also diminished clients' view of the overall value of the practice. I was often amazed how much more proficient a veterinarian I was at only 2 plus years out of school than some of the single practitioners I covered for that were 15 - 20 years out of school. Given the choice, clients that have a long standing relationship with a practice would far rather have a procedure done there versus being referred out to a referral center they are not familiar with and would pay 4 times the amount.

Expanding on that, clients like the one stop shop model of veterinary clinics where beyond high level, affordable pet health care, they can also have their pets groomed, and leave them for boarding . Single doctor practices rarely provided this.

With all of these things considered, my plan was to go for the "fixer-upper" single doctor practice, right out of the gate add value in the practice bringing with me the unusually expansive scope of skills for a veterinarian just under 3 years of practice that resulted from working in a good practice and expanding my experience per diem; the phase of my career that I call "veterinarian boot camp." In addition to this, I would gradually add exponential value to the practice by adding the other ancillary services to support growing into a multi doctor practice.

I did not have to look very long, as I quickly found what seemed to be the ideal practice to carry out my plan.

Chapter 27 - "Every block of stone has a statue inside it and it is the task of the sculptor to discover it" - *Michelangelo*

The practice was called Maybeck Animal Hospital, Brevard County, Florida's first animal hospital, first built in 1952 and was rumored to have seen the pets of some of the original Mercury 7 astronauts. Despite its long history, the practice curiously had remained a one doctor practice for most of its history, at the time on its second owner, Dr. Constance Mengering who had purchased the practice in 1981.

Within a week of finding the practice and having reached out to the listing agent, I flew down to West Melbourne, FL, to meet Dr. Mengering and check out the practice. During my tour, I saw a curiously laid out practice with very interesting architecture.

The building was brick face with wood shingle roof facade. The side of the building that faced the parking lot was a screened in porch where a refrigerator and corpse freezer was located. The walls of the inside of the building were constructed of wood paneling, reminiscent of the preferred decor of the finished basements of homes up north in the 1980's. Also reminiscent of the 80's were certain sections covered in wallpaper.

I cannot realistically get into the lay out of the hospitals in writing, but beyond the waiting room, reception and the hallway with exam rooms, it reminded me of a rat maze with a bit of a haphazard flow to it. I learned that this was the result of additions being built over time in such a manner that they did not compromise the main load bearing concrete block base construction and foundation.

The characteristic of the commercial real estate of the practice that really stuck out to me was that it had a gravel parking lot. Dr. Mengering informed me that with such a high water table and heavy rains in Florida during the rainy season, the engineering necessary to either hook into the main storm drain of Route 192 (the main road the building was situated on) or build a retention pond for drainage was too cost prohibitive to have the parking lot paved.

Still, the broker's description of the building in the listing was surprisingly accurate: "...dated, but quite functional with 3 full exam rooms providing opportunity to grow beyond one doctor." It was not the prettiest thing I had ever seen but it was functional and had potential.

The area itself also had great potential. Route 192 is a road that runs all the way from the beach (Indialantic Beach, about 4 miles east and over a causeway from the practice) to Kissimmee where Disney and other theme parks are just outside of Orlando in Central Florida. The practice was in a business district walking distance from a Target, Kinkos, McDonalds, Arby's, and TGI Fridays, directly situated between an Olive Garden and Wendy's.

A bit inland from the beach, West Melbourne was in the beginning of transition from a primarily rural region of cattle and sod farms to brand new subdivisions. Farmers that had inherited land that was in their families for generations were finding it more lucrative to sell off tracts of land to contractors for development than to farm the land. The contractors loved it because there was an appetite for people to live in West Melbourne given its lower cost than beachside real estate yet still in reasonably close proximity to the beach; and better protection from hurricanes being a little further inland to boot.

Located on the southern end of the Space Coast, technology companies, primarily defense, space and aeronautics companies like Northrop Grumman, General Electric, Harris, Rockville Collins, and Boeing were expanding operations in West Melbourne. This was increasingly attracting corporate families, the parents of which worked in engineering, finance, and middle and executive management.

Despite this, there was a very country vibe still very prevalent among the people. Dr. Mengering herself raised llamas and ostriches on her 10 acre farm and her husband was an avid alligator hunter. It would be an adjustment for me but having lived in the rust belt in Illinois during clinics and married to a country girl, this would not be completely foreign to me.

My mind was made up; this would be the practice I would buy. Dr. Mengering turned out to be a wonderfully amicable person and our negotiations were pretty seamless, easily meeting halfway on price and other negotiable aspects of the practice and real estate purchase. We came to terms and Melissa and I submitted our request to our broker and held our breath as we awaited the answer on the financing for the purchase. We got our approval 2 weeks later.

Chapter 28 - "The journey of a thousand miles begins with one step." - *Lao Tzu*

After having gotten approval for the practice purchase financing, the tasks ahead of Melissa and I were so numerous and monumental that we almost did not know where to start: study and sit for the Florida State Veterinary Board licensing exam, sell our house in NY, find and purchase a house in Florida, start packing up our home, and constantly having conference calls with our broker, accountant, and attorney; all while still working our full time jobs.

Melissa is an amazing planner and she is incredibly resourceful, but she has never had the appetite or patience for having to will things to get done. This does not apply to home life, of course, as there is no project that Melissa will fail to give anything less than 110% of her attention to. When I state "willing things to get done," I am referring to calling plumbers to fix our overflowing septic tank, arguing with the utility company that over billed us, calling a company to get our heating fixed, etc. (these are a few of the things I actually had to deal with during the time we lived in our home in Huntington).

Thus, the task of dealing with every aspect of our pending transactions fell mostly on me. The one thing we did do together was to fly to Brevard County to for a weekend to shop for a new home. Without a lot of time we had to cram 20 home visits within a 36 hour period before settling on the right house. We chose a 3 bedroom home in a community known as Viera.

Viera was about a 25 - 30 minute drive north of the practice we were about to purchase, but it was a brand new area having been designed and built on former cattle ranch land (basically a further advanced version of where West Melbourne was headed). All of the homes and local architecture were brand new with the latest hurricane safety regulations with not one visible power line above ground.

A lot of the population was northern transplants that had settled in the area to work at Kennedy Space Center or one of the expanding technology companies. Our goal was to eventually start a family so we also chose Viera for it's A rated schools.

Among other really neat perks about Viera was that government regulations mandated that a certain amount of land had to be set aside for conservation. The community we settled on surrounded an 80 acre region of wildlife preserve full of wild boar, lakes teaming with local fish and gators, bobcats, and a huge assortment of birdlife.

The entire town was interconnected with golf cart paths that wove in and out of the preserves and went all the way to The Avenue, the name of the town center where all of the shops, restaurants, movie theaters, and bars were. Also golf cart accessible was the Space Coast Stadium where the Washington Nationals had their spring training every year. This was a very cool place to live for a young couple.

Upon returning to Long Island, we had gotten a serious offer on our home there. This was ever important because per the banks' mandates for both our new home and business purchases were contingent upon the sale of our home in Long Island. We had until December 15, 2004 to close on our home sale in NY, move, then close on our new home and practice in Florida. By this time it was already late October, 2004.

Melissa and I were pleasantly surprised to learn that in the short time we owned our home; it had gone up in value considerably so we would be moving to Florida with a decent sum of money to sustain us as we grew the practice to a point that it would provide us a more comfortable income. We were also very happy that the people we had accepted the offer from were a very nice young couple who had just gotten married and were in love with all of the touches we had put into the house (including a duck pond in the backyard - my personal favorite touch).

Closing on a home in NY, however, is a painfully slow process in comparison to other states, necessitating three attorneys: one for the seller, one for the buyer, and one for the title company. We were going to be cutting it uncomfortably close for our December 15th deadline.

Things were proceeding very smoothly when one week before Thanksgiving, the title company found a red flag preventing us from getting clean title. There was a small road just behind our backyard with a few homes on it. Quite oddly, given the original zoning, the road was actually owned by a man who lived in Queens.

The sticky point was that the man had run a fence along the back property of the backyards of all of the homes on our adjacent street and the fence line encroached 12 inches onto our property creating a barrier preventing us from getting a clean title, an essential step in selling the home. I told my attorney that I would simply take a chainsaw to the fence to solve the problem, but he informed me that would not settle it because the fence was there for longer than the common law statute, so technically the 12 inches of land on which the fence encroached upon and the ownership of the fence itself, would be in dispute and the litigation to settle the matter could take months to even years! The previous title company we had used to purchase the home did not catch this, so Melissa and I were completely blindsided with this. After all of this preparation and work, finding the perfect practice and having ¾ of our home already packed up in boxes, Melissa and were on the verge of being stuck in Long Island indefinitely.

The man in Queens who owned the road was rumored by several of our neighbors to be painfully obstinate, apparently not having given an inch in matters such as this with several other households in the neighborhood that bordered his road and his fencing. The rumors were confirmed after our attorney had reached out to him to appeal to a sense of empathy for all that was riding on the sale of a young couple's home; to find a timely and fair solutions without getting courts involved. He refused, stating that he would see us in court.

By this time, Thanksgiving had arrived and my entire family was now living in Florida. We spent Thanksgiving evening with the family of Melissa's employers at their family farm house in Northport. As kind of them as it was to invite us and in the quaint farmhouse decor, I had a very hard time finding any cheer in the occasion. I had to consume double the amount of wine to remotely enjoy it.

With our real estate agent, title company attorney, and our personal attorney off for the long weekend, it would be a painful wait to see what our options were if any with just 2 plus weeks away from our deadline to close. On Monday, we got our answer; the title company told us that we had two options: fight it out in court with the man in Queens or approach the sellers and see if they would still purchase the home without clean title. The former would kill the purchase of the clinic, our home in Florida, and keep us in Long Island for the foreseeable future. The latter was a long shot, as purchasing the home would leave it so the buyers would run into the same problem if they in turn went to sell the home. It would be their task to settle this problem with the owner of the road and fence themselves.

In the process of showing the home and negotiating the purchase price of the home, Melissa and I had come to be very friendly with the couple intending to buy our home. I had the husband's cell phone and asked him to please come by after work, as there was an issue with the title they needed to make a decision on. Everything was riding on this conversation.

They came over and I told them the situation as I showed them the fence. The wife said, "I'll be damned if the purchase of my new home is going to be held up by some asshole on a power trip over owning a a stupid rickety old fence!" Her husband agreed and they decided to proceed with the purchase and deal with the issue themselves. From their perspective, they had plenty of time, as they intended to live in the home for many years and raise a family there.

I felt like the weight of the world was lifted off my shoulders and the sense of relief I felt at that moment could not be overstated. When I told Melissa, she felt the same.

We had the house fully packed up on December 6, 2004, including our bedroom set, so Melissa and I slept on blankets and pillows on the basement floor for our last night in the home, the only room with soft carpeting. Despite the sleeping arrangement our spirits were high. In the morning, we awoke to a cold, miserable day with rain and sleet and closed at 9 AM. We packed up our 3 dogs, cat, and personal belongings that did not go with the moving truck into our two cars and followed one another out of NY for good. Before boarding the cars, we both lamented that we will never have to wake up to cold and sleet ever again.

Having to close on the purchase of our home in Florida on the morning of December 8, we had to make the 18 hour drive straight through without stopping to overnight. By the time we reached Jacksonville, I was so sleepy I had to consume large amounts of coffee, blasting the music, and occasionally slapping myself and we were still 3 hours away from Viera.

We arrived at my parent's place in the wee hours of the morning to rest briefly and get cleaned up for the closing. After all we had been through; there would be one more snag before we could own our new home in Viera: the wire transfer from the bank for the down payment had not yet cleared!

The seller's real estate agent we encountered was yet another obstinate ass and refused to give us the keys to move in, even though the money from our money from the mortgage company had already cleared and the bank transfer for our down payment was listed as "in process." The moving truck was set to arrive that afternoon and with another house to hit right after ours, the movers could not wait 1-2 business days that it might take for our wire transfer to fully clear (that was the best estimate that the bank would give us). We would have to rent a storage unit for the movers to put our furniture and boxes in, then hire another local company to move it all again once the wire cleared. On top of this, I was processing all of this on no sleep for the past 30 hours!

Ultimately, Mom and Dad came to the rescue. After 2 hours on the phone, my parents managed to get the money wired from one of their money market accounts and we would pay them back once our wire arrived. The movers had not yet arrived when we got to the house following closing. All I wanted to do was pass out on the floor overcome with physical and mental exhaustion. My wife, on the other hand, had also not slept, but instead of being tired got hyperactive and slap happy. She decided that she did not like the color of the bedroom, went to Lowes to buy paint, and painted the bedroom while I slept until the movers arrived.

Waking in our first morning living in a Florida winter was wonderful, sipping on our coffee, me wearing only a hoodie and shorts on our screened in porch on a sunny, 62 degree morning. We made it! Just the practice closing remained. Melissa and I had paid the practice a visit to make sure the appointment book was set up for the schedule breakdown of procedures and appointments that I would be working the day after closing. I also spoke with the current practice manager and had her start setting up the entire vendor and reference lab accounts so that we could hit the ground running with no interruption in patient care and workflow.

December 15, 2019 came pretty quickly. The business closing ended up being seamless. That night, my parents took the whole family out to the Chart House restaurant on the water to celebrate. My Mom had custom menus made for the occasion that said, "Congratulations to Roger and Melissa on their new clinic. May God bless them with many years success." It was amazing!

Chapter 29 - "Find your place on the planet. Dig in and take responsibility from there..." - *Gary Snyder*

The Central East Coast of Florida was a slower pace of life full of very nice people.   In comparison to New York where I was practicing in veterinarian paradise (from the perspective of cost not being a hindrance to the quality of medicine I could practice), my new Florida home was a very diverse, eclectic mix of people. 2004 in my area was in the midst of a housing boom (that would later be a giant, exploding bubble..but that is for another chapter) and attracting many investors and northern transplants like me seeking lower taxes and cost of living with the added perk of no winter. There were also people that had grown up here and were very much like the southerners and rust belt people I had encountered in veterinary school, that identified themselves as "Florida crackers."

Personally, the change of pace, culture, and demographic was fine for me. I had lived in such a diversity of places by this point that I learned that people are people, and while we may have different outlooks based on cultural difference and how we were raised, we really are the same deep inside. Professionally, however, the differences from New York took some getting used to.

The staff that I inherited generally represented more the grassroots generational section of the population. The techs worked at a certain pace regardless of how full the waiting room was or how much we were running behind, whereas Melissa and I, she a university trained tech and me a veterinarian that had come fresh from high paced, high end practices worked with a greater sense of urgency.

It is not to say that the staff was lackadaisical in any way with regard to upping their urgency and pace for very sick, injured, or critical patients and no matter how full our book was, they would not hesitate to get a very sick or injured patient in even it meant double and triple hooking me. These people cared a great deal about the animals, and that side I appreciated.

The lack of urgency was more with the non-critical, routine visits; especially the well visits where the animals were not sick. They really did not have all that much concern about making these clients wait. The clients that had grown up in the area tended to not get too miffed about wait times, while the northern transplants tended to get impatient. Melissa and I stressed about it because we had just come from spending nearly 3 years in a "time is money" culture.

I can have a bit of a potty mouth at times, something that the staff was clearly not used to from the previous owner. One particular technician named Beth, a devout Evangelical Christian, could not hide her cringe every time I uttered profanity. I tried my best to keep it in check, but swearing during times of stress I have read is a clinically proven way of effectively relieving stress. Case in point, there was far more swearing in the ER I worked at than anywhere else I ever worked.

I generally got on well with the clients themselves. While I talked a bit fast for some of the native Floridians and hand gestured more than they were used to, they had confidence in my knowledge and skill in veterinary medicine and especially liked not having to be referred out to specialists as often for procedures as the previous owner did. The northern transplants, especially those from NY and NJ, I of course meshed with extremely well. They were just tickled to have one of their own as their family vet in Florida.

As time went on, Melissa and I were starting to get very subconscious about the 80's style wood paneling throughout the clinic but being new owners and not having much capital to have it professionally made over; we were kind of stuck with it. Then, ever the resourceful one, Melissa came up with a great idea. She suggested that we paint over the paneling with texture paint that leaves a rough, almost plaster-like creviced texture to the walls that would hide the grooves of the paneling; then once dry, cover that with a coat of primer and two coats of a light colored paint (an off white color).

With all of the time we were spending in the practice of medicine and learning to run a business, we made the decision that we would save time by just doing the areas where the clients could actually see the decor: waiting room, reception, and hallway leading to the exam rooms, exam rooms, and bathroom.

For two weekends, after we were done seeing patients after Noon on Saturday, we got to work relentlessly well into the night on Saturday and all day and night Sunday. We ordered food in and worked virtually non-stop trying to get as much done before open of business on Monday.

Toward the end of the first Sunday, we had reached the primer phase of our painting. At one point, Melissa came up to me complaining that she could not feel her lips. I stopped painting and noted eerily that I could not feel mine either! In fact, I felt really weird in general.

We realized that the oil based primer we had chosen was giving off fumes that were intoxicating us. We went outside for fresh air and soon started to feel better. At that point we stopped work and ran to Home Depot to buy gas masks to wear for the rest of the priming phase.

When we were done, the difference was amazing. Apparently the awful decor of wood paneling did not escape the notice of many of our clients, as many commented on how much nicer the place looked. Little did they know that the paneling was very much still there, just cleverly covered over with texture paint. It is still there to this day, only now repainted over with a more beach-themed light blue.

By 2007, the business could (just barely) afford to have an exterior makeover and the rest of the interior where we worked finished professionally by a contractor. There would be no more intoxicating ourselves with primer or having to virtually move into the clinic for weekends to complete the work.

He simply did the same that we did, even found it a quite clever solution to the paneling problem (go Melissa!). For the outside, he replaced the unsightly, decaying wooden facade around the roof with a blue metal facade and painted the brick face a light beige color.

Once again, the clients really noticed and commented constantly after it was done. My Mom who was now the practice manager, was covering the front desk one day shortly after the project was finished and a client commented to her that the building instantly seemed to better reflect the high level of medicine that Maybeck Animal Hospital offered.

Speaking of my Mom, she had been working in the practice for the first year to help manage the front desk staff, while also working to gradually taking over the day to day interactions with vendors, pharmaceutical reps, reference laboratories, and finding the cheapest way to get things fixed when they broke down, a frequent occurrence in the old building, shiny new roof facade and paint job notwithstanding.

Within a short time, I named her practice manager to also take over the HR side of the business, something that I particularly did not enjoy. My Mom's background was very well suited for the position having been a very successful realtor and later the manager of a large and posh spa in Summit, NJ. Plus, she was for all intents and purposes retired by this time and did it more for love and pride in her son than anything. And who can you trust more than Mom?

Maybeck became very much a family affair. My father who retired from working on the finance side of Merck Pharmaceuticals at only age 55 had a bit of time on his hands, so he offered to reconcile our bank statements each month. Having been a financial executive for a Fortune 500 company, I could not find anyone more meticulous to do this job.

My sister who by mid-2006 was in the midst of transitioning to another career opportunity even spent the better part of a year working as part of the front desk staff. A naturally extroverted and empathetic person, the clients just loved her genuineness.

Personally, Melissa and I were very happy. My parents lived across the street from a young couple, both veterinarians that were also new to the area and they introduced us. We made fast friends and grew our social circle, not surprisingly, a bunch of veterinarians and their spouses.

Ever the active outdoor person, I just fell in love with living in Florida. I surfed 3-4 times per week. If I knew there was going to be a solid swell on a work day, I would strap my board on my truck before leaving for work and go surf over lunch time. My buddy Matt, one of the vets that I met through my parents, was an avid boater who took us out cruising and fishing all the time.

Life was also awesome for my dogs, Tiffany, Lulu, and my wife's Yorkie Bear. They were outdoors all the time with rarely lousy weather to imprison them indoors. We were a very happy little furry family, happily building a business and life together.

But I would soon experience the relevance of the famous quote from the line in The Grateful Dead's "Uncle John's Band," "...when life looks like easy street there is danger at your door."

Chapter 30 - "Dogs come into our lives to teach us about love, they depart to teach us about loss. A new dog never replaces an old dog, it merely expands the heart. If you have loved many dogs your heart is very big." — *Erica Jong*

One day I noticed that my beloved Labrador Retriever Tiffany seemed a bit thin over her mid back and I could see the bumps in her spine called spinous processes. By this time Tiffany was 8 years old and in her life I had repaired both of her knees having torn her ACL in each knee. With everything else normal, I assumed that the loss of muscle over her back was simply the result of some loss of lean muscle from the onset of arthritis from her past injuries.

Still unusual for her age and given that she was so sound on her limbs and seemingly healthy in every way, I ran a battery of tests on Tiffany which turned up nothing. I put her on a veterinary grade joint health supplement and a top quality senior diet and hoped that would help improve her body condition.

One day when I was petting her, I felt a few big lumps on one side of her neck, then found that it was the same on the other side. Knowing immediately that these were enlarged lymph nodes, I checked the rest of the peripheral lymph nodes that are palpable on physical examination and they were all equally enlarged. I suddenly knew why Tiffany's body condition was deteriorating...she had lymphoma.

Lymphoma is short for lymphosarcoma, which is a cancer of the lymphatic system of the body. Because the lymphatic system interconnects all of the body's organ systems, it is a non-surgical cancer that responds only to chemotherapy. Despite being devastated at my discovery, I certainly was not without hope. I had done a medical oncology rotation in veterinary school and practiced quite a bit of cancer medicine working in NY.

Chemotherapy in pets is far different from chemotherapy in people because the primary goal of chemotherapy in people is far different from that in pets. With people, the goal is eradication of the cancer for a temporary (hopefully) sacrifice in quality of life. The ultimate prize is longevity and human doctors will bring people to the brink of death to achieve that.

In veterinary medicine, only a brief sacrifice in quality of life is acceptable. Without quality of life, our ethics prevent us from recommending courses of treatment that will cause a long term sacrifice in quality of life. As such, the goal of cancer medicine in pets is to dial back the doses of chemotherapy that will find that perfect medium that provides maximum cancer remission while maintaining quality of life and providing some additional longevity.

In Tiffany's case, once I confirmed her diagnosis of lymphoma via simple needle aspirate of a couple of her swollen lymph nodes, I learned that she had the most treatable form of lymphoma that responded favorably to a generally well tolerated chemotherapy regimen called the Wisconsin protocol. This protocol provides an average remission rate of 18 months and I had many cases in NY that were still in remission far beyond that. There most certainly was hope!

Tiffany was such a sweet girl and the weekly IV treatments did not bother her one bit and she had always come to work with me anyway. Her remission started immediately after the first treatment and she was back to normal, swimming in the pool, gaining weight, and all her lymph nodes back to normal size. In the first few weeks, Tiffany showed no negative effects from the chemotherapy whatsoever.

During this time, a beautiful 4 month old Yellow Lab puppy came in unable to use his front left leg. It was basically limp and he was in terrible pain. I asked the family what happened and they told me the other dog in the home fell on top of the puppy during play.

Their other dog had been to the clinic a couple of times and I looked him up to find that he was about a 45 pound dog. When I took x-rays the puppy's limp limb, I found that he had a severe displaced fracture of both of the major long bones that comprise the elbow (the humerus and ulna. Essentially, both bones were in three pieces and across the growth plates.

It occurred to me that the explanation for such as severe fracture did not add up (I had never seen such a severe injury that did not involve a major trauma). The explanation for the fracture seemed very suspicious to me, especially given that the Lab puppy this age was only slightly smaller than the dog that supposedly caused this by falling on top of him. Although the rest of the entirety of the family was present for what would ultimately be two visits, the father whose name was listed as the primary on the account never attended or even called me. I had no proof of abuse, but my radar was up for certain.

It also occurred to me that a fracture with this degree of complication required the expertise of a surgical specialist. Given the degree of displacement, multiple bone fragments, and very important nerves in the region integral for use of the limb, as far as I had expanded my orthopedic surgical skills, I would still refer a case like this to a specialist even today. I therefore placed a splint on the limb, dispensed pain medication for the puppy, and recommended an immediate referral to the specialist at the local veterinary referral center.

I was very concerned that the family would have difficulty following through with a specialist. The puppy to date had never been seen by a veterinarian, had never had one single vaccine, or had been tested or treated for parasites. Case in point, after he came out of his sedation that was necessary to take x-rays and splint his limb, he vomited up a wad of worms.

A full week went by and I had heard nothing from the puppy's owners and I could not get him out of my mind, so I called them. The mother of the family told me that they went to the specialist but could not afford the quote they were given. She further elaborated that they had to borrow the money just for the visit at my clinic and for the specialist's consultation fee. Even worse, the splint I put on that was meant to be very temporary was still on!

I made the instantaneous decision to offer to have the puppy signed over to the clinic. Even if this family could scrounge up the money for the surgery, I had no confidence that they would comply with the very rigid restrictions and rehabilitation that would be necessary for such an intense and highly technical repair. They had proven that they really had no idea of what it entails to properly care for a dog period, and there was still my intuition that there was abuse involved (I never did hear from the husband). I offered this option to the owner for the sake of the puppy and she agreed.

With three dogs (one of which was undergoing cancer therapy) and two cats, the last thing I needed was another dog, so my plan was to have the clinic cover the cost of the surgery, foster the puppy through his recovery, and find him a good forever home.

I telephoned the referral center and spoke with their surgical specialist, Dr. Jeff Christiansen. I told him the circumstances and he informed me that this was among the hardest types of fractures to repair and the prognosis for full use of the limb was guarded. I went ahead and scheduled the procedure.

The puppy was dropped off and I was horrified to see that the splint was filthy, covered in urine, and, and was emitting a terrible smell. We had to cut it off, soak the limb with antiseptic, and reapply a clean splint to prepare for dropping the puppy off the next day for surgery.

I dropped the puppy off for surgery at 8 AM. By 2 PM, I still had not yet heard any updates so I called the referral center for a status update. The receptionist patched me through to the speaker phone in the operating room and Dr. Christiansen informed me that he was just about done, that the procedure had taken him 5 plus hours! I was to pick up Bernie the next day.

When my wife and I went to the referral center to pick up Bernie, two things struck us. First, we were astonished at the post-operative x-rays. It appeared that the puppy had a bionic elbow.

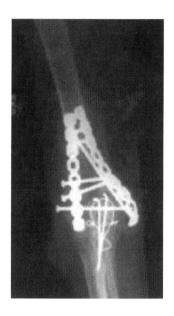

Second, as we entered the treatment area, the puppy started barking like crazy when he saw me, as if saying, "Daddy!" This did not escape the attention of the techs who noted that with all the narcotic pain medication he was on, that was the only time all day he had even lifted his head, let alone stand up in his body cast and bark.

On another positive note, Dr. Christiansen told me that provided there was no complication and everything healed, 80%of the growth of the upper comes from the growth plate closer to the shoulder, so by this age, there should not be a significant discrepancy in the length of this limb in comparison to the others.

We took the puppy home to introduce him to his new temporary home.

Yellow Lab puppy still to be named 2006

We could not leave the puppy unnamed and we really did not like his previous name, so we named him Bernie, after the New York Yankees great Center Fielder. I was a lifelong Yankees fan and while living in New York and taking Melissa to a few Yankees games, she became a pretty avid fan. We subsequently got into the habit of naming our pets after our favorite Yankee players (we had a cat named Mo after Mariano Rivera and currently have a cat named Yogi after Yogi Berra).

Bernie was so different than Tiffany. While Tiffany was so intelligent, self-trained, and refined, Bernie was not so smart and a complete goofball, but as loveable and cuddly as any dog could be. He fit right into our happy furry household as if he had always been there and made himself quite at home.

In the process of my follow up visits with Dr. Jeff Christiansen who performed the brilliant work on Bernie's arm, he and I became good friends, eventually socializing regularly together with our wives who got along splendidly.

A few weeks into rehabilitating Bernie, I found myself becoming really attached to him and I could not bear the thought of letting him go. He was also very attached to me as if he had been my dog all along and I could not bear the thought of rehoming him especially after all he had been through. So now on top of spending a large sum of money on a dog that was not even ours, I had to go to my wife and float the idea of keeping Bernie permanently.

One night I approached her about it and she smiled and simply said, "Honey, I knew the moment that we picked up Bernie from the emergency clinic that he was going nowhere. He is your dog." My wife is awesome!

Eventually Bernie graduated to a soft bandage and within 8 weeks was completely healed with no limp at all. The only side effect of his injury was his front paw turned out sideways when he walked and trotted which comically added to his already goofy character. What shocked us was how large he was getting.

At 75 pounds, Tiffany was a large female Lab but by 6 months of age, Bernie was already 45 pounds (dogs will generally ultimately grow to double their 6 month weight). He was going to be a big boy!

Roger and Bernie Welton 2006

Tiffany's treatments in the meantime were proceeding
phenomenally well but about 6 weeks into her treatment she
developed diarrhea and shortly after had blood in it. I chalked it
up to a simple chemotherapy complication that affected her gut
negatively and initiated treatment for ulcerative colitis

immediately. Unfortunately, despite my best efforts and throwing every medication I could at her issue, she continued to get worse then eventually started vomiting and would not eat.

My wife and I ran continuous fluids and broke out the big gun anti-nausea intravenous medications and nothing seemed to help her. One night, Tiffany could not get comfortable to lie down and sleep and kept getting up and pacing because she had so much pain in her abdomen. At around 11 PM, she gave me such a look of desperation that I decided I could no longer put her through this and in tears told Melissa that I was taking her to the clinic to put her to sleep. It was the most painful decision of my life but I had nothing left in my medical arsenal to ease her suffering.

Melissa mandated that she come with me knowing how hard it was doing to be for me. Unbeknownst to me, she had called my parents and told them and I arrived at the clinic near midnight to find my parents, my sister, my brother, and his wife who had all come to say goodbye to Tiffany and comfort me through my grief. While they had come to love the legendary Tiffdog as we called her, they knew that she was a part of my soul.

I hugged Tiffany close to me and kissed her as Melissa administered the injection through the IV catheter she already had in place and just like that, one month before her ninth birthday, my beloved Tiffdog was gone.

While my life had led me to so many new places and experiences, love gained and love lost, Tiffany was always my constant, my little rock that made me always feel I was at home as long as she was with me. It was the most devastated I had ever felt in my life to date.

When I got home that night, I looked at Bernie and had a similar feeling I had when I lost Waldo; that any dog after him would be short changed because I could not possibly love another dog the same. In tears told him that I was sorry that I will not likely ever love him as much as I loved Tiffany, then I hugged him and cried on his shoulder. He licked my ear in return, not in his goofy puppy way but gently as if he sensed the grief I was feeling.

For the next few weeks I stayed away from home as much as possible. I threw myself into work and saw as many patients as I could. Helping other pets kept my mind off Tiffany. Like Tiffany, I brought Bernie to work with me every day.

I spent so much time at work that I would take naps on the Lazy Boy recliner in my office and Bernie got in the habit of jumping in, cuddling and napping with me in the chair. My staff thought it was hilarious, especially as Bernie ultimately would grow to 87 pounds and still cuddled on the Lazy Boy with me.

Beyond work, I took Bernie everywhere with me that I could and always to my relatives' houses when invited over. I did not realize it as it was occurring, but as I put the raw grief of losing Tiffany behind me, Bernie was playing a primary role in helping me be able to move on. He helped to fill the void that Tiffany had left behind and was my inseparable companion. My sister would later share with me that after Tiffany died, my Mom said, "Thank God Bernie came into Roger's life at just the right time."

I grew to adore Bernie and love him as much as I loved Tiffany. He did not replace her, as he was a totally different dog. He took up residence in a new place in my heart.

Bernie Williams Welton 2006

Now please do not get the idea that I am snubbing Lulu, my rescue dog from Illinois. Lulu, you have to understand, was a Border Collie mix of sorts that was sweet and gentle, but she was a bit independent. She would far prefer to be outside in the backyard for hours at a time chasing squirrels than being inside snuggling with me. We loved Lulu for who she was but she was a free spirit unlike my Labradors who would not leave my hip.

Still, I missed my Tiffdog but after several weeks, I could speak about her without welling up with tears and actually smile at some of our great memories. I decided I would honor her memory by starting a charity fund called the "Tiffany Fund" for owners of sick or injured dogs who did not have the money to pay for their care. The fund received direct donations online, in a donation box at the reception desk, and made money on candy machine sales in the waiting room. It was wonderful to see pets getting well needed care in the name of my beloved girl.

That fund still exists today and has been responsible for saving countless furry lives.

Tiffany Welton 2003 Huntington, NY

Tiffany Welton 2006 (just before she got sick)

Chapter 31 - "Don't hate the media, become the media" — *Jello Biafra*

In my first years of clinical practice, while there were not big social media outlets, there were community forums for discussion and chain emails that made the rounds of many an inbox. Thus began the beginning of the age of instantaneous information and in many cases, MISinformation.

I was still in NY when I started occasionally hearing from clients about some of the most outrageous ideas people had that they were getting off the internet and much disillusionment, sometimes not being able to talk them out of their opinion that they may have gotten from some nameless, faceless person on a pet forum.

I heard about vaccines causing far more harm than the good they do to protect health. I heard about people feeding their dogs raw chicken wings as the staple diet. It was requested of me to perform spays but leave the ovaries because dogs "need their hormones." I was informed by some pet owners that they would not take my nutritional advice because veterinarians are not taught nutrition in veterinary school. For other pet owners, they accepted that veterinarians got nutrition training but went on the conspiracy theory that all of our education was spoon fed to us and funded by pet food companies who we were then in the tank for….then as practitioners were showered with perks and lavish vacations to promote the feeding of their poison to pets. I could go on here, and the list of outlandish ideas has grown exponentially since the advent of social media.

In the course of my busy day dealing with legitimately sick animals and the majority of people that had enough faith in my medicine to accept my recommendations over a groomer or breeder they had corresponded with on a pet forum; I found myself becoming increasingly impatient with the naysayers that took the internet as veterinary medical gospel. I found that sitting in the room with these people and having to politely explain the absurdity of their beliefs borne of nonsensical misinformation from people that have no training or business giving veterinary medical advice was a colossal waste of my time.

At the same time, I saw the increasing power of media to spread good information and to be a strong counter-force to push back against the era of "alternative facts" with no basis in science and medicine. On the human side, I saw sites like Web-MD that had wide ranging articles written by real experts but did not see its equivalent with any real credibility on the veterinary side.

This resulted in my creation of Web-DVM (WebDVM.Net) in 2005 where it started with a series of disease articles with signs to look for, diagnosis, treatment, and prevention. Once I had a solid base of disease articles, I added a blog that was information on issues I thought pet owners needed to be educated on based on my experiences in day to day clinical practice. Sometimes my blog would be a venting session as I anonymously wrote about cases where clients were inclined to pick an internet recommendation over that of my own and why their opinions were so misguided.

In this manner, not only did not get the true message out and spread accurate information, the blog became a cathartic release for me and I found myself writing constantly. What's more, I was accumulating such a database of articles that often when I had a difficult client bent on believing the internet over my recommendation, I would not have to waste my time and just say, "You know what, I just happen to have written an article on this very topic, give me your email address and I will send you the link. Read it and call me if you change your mind."

It was amazing that just being a writer on the internet was often enough to change hearts and minds. Never mind my veterinary degree and clinical experience; if I am writing on the internet, I must know what I am talking about!

Over time I added a virtual "symptom checker" that gave pet owners an idea of what could be going on with their pet determined through a series of prompts (it took me a whole summer to create this algorithm). After gaining a rather substantial online following, I later learned that I could monetize the site by placing Google and other ads throughout the site that provided ad content that was relevant to the material being presented. In this manner, my visitors maintained free access to information while I could actually derive income from my media work.

At first, the site may have brought in at most $50 per month but over time became a fairly substantial source of income that was crucial as I took as little money as possible out of the clinic to reinvest in growing my practice and would be further financially strapped by future circumstances beyond my control (stay tuned for life as a veterinarian after the financial crash of 2008!).

Around 2008/2009, I had begun to notice a new internet phenomenon called "podcasting," where anyone with a platform could create internet radio shows right from their computers with a modest investment in audio equipment and software. Hence was born the podcast, "Veterinary Advice, Animal News and Views." The show would air on a network called BlogTalkRadio and within an hour of airing would post on ITunes.

For the first few years, it was just me alone going on the air and talking about topics I deemed relevant. I would select a few email questions or comments from listeners per week and address them on the air. Also, streaming the podcast through my Web-DVM website, the podcast gained a following in a short period of time.

The beauty of podcasts is that listeners can tune in live or listen on archive on either the podcast network or via ITunes at their convenience. Thus, not having to interrupt their busy schedules to tune in, listeners may take in episodes while on the treadmill or commuting to and from work. In fact, the majority of my listeners today (as of the writing of this book, each of my episodes brings in about 10,000 listens) tune in by archive.

What's more, the episodes remain archived with their key words on the show page indefinitely. Subsequently, a person searching the internet for subject matter I had podcasted on years ago could come across an episode during their search and suddenly I have a new fan from a topic I discussed long ago.

Around 2014, an actual veterinarian sent in an email comment about a particularly ranty article I had written at Web-DVM that she took pleasure in as my words echoed the same frustrations she dealt with on this particular topic in clinical practice. She told me that she wanted to high five me through the computer which I found hilarious. She also informed me that she had her own blog as well that was both cathartic for her but also spread information in a very lay terminology and cheeky format where pet owners could feel that they were interacting with the veterinarian friend they never had. Dr. Karen Louis called her blog VetChick.com which went perfectly with the presentation she had intended

As I perused Karen's articles I saw a keen intelligence in her writing but also a wit and tongue in cheek humor that differed from my writing. We were both effective communicators but in very different manners and I thought our styles complemented one another very well.

Karen was also a 2004 graduate of University of Illinois, College of Veterinary Medicine where I had done my year of clinical rotations and finished in 2002. She lived and practiced in Illinois, the land of my wife and family and I just saw too much coincidence in all of this to not follow up on finding mutual opportunity.

I floated the idea of Karen guest co-hosting a podcast episode with me on the subject of one of her hilarious blog posts about a disturbing and growing trend at the time of pet owners coming to believe in treating their pets with coconut oil for any number of conditions. This new supposed magical elixir of life not only usually did not work for anything pet owners were trying to treat, but it also often had some serious unwanted health consequences.

We co-hosted via video Skype which made it easy to co-cost from thousands of miles away. In our first episode, we hit it off as if we had been co-hosting together for years with an uncanny chemistry born out of our contrasting but complementary styles. It was also more fun to podcast with such a clever and intelligent veterinarian. I asked her if she wanted to make it a permanent gig, she said yes and has been co-hosting with me ever since.

Chapter 32 - The two most important days of your life is the day you are born and the day you find out why. - *Mark Twain*

After more than a year of trying to conceive, in November of 2007, my wife and I found out that she was pregnant with our first child. From the moment I first saw the child's miniscule heartbeat on the ultrasound when he looked like little more than a little bean, I was encompassed by a love that I had never felt before. From that moment on, I knew my purpose in life was first and foremost to dutifully dedicate my life to my child's welfare.

It was such an exciting time as Melissa and I got past the early period and we announced the pregnancy to my parents at Thanksgiving dinner with a card and a picture of our child's ultrasound in it. My Mom cried with joy and while my Dad has never been much of a crier, I could see that his eyes were glazed over with threatening tears. For my wife and me it was the best Thanksgiving of our lives. We would soon find out that our child was to be a boy and we excitedly converted our guest bedroom to a nursery in a boy's decor.

Everything was progressing smoothly when in the last trimester, it was discovered by routine ultrasound that, while our son's head and brain were growing adequately, his body was not keeping pace. His OBGYN, Dr. Victor Benezra called this phenomenon brain sparing intrauterine growth restriction which meant that the child was not growing for some reason but as a natural protective mechanism, the existing growth was focused more toward the head to protect and maintain brain development first and foremost. Still, this was a serious concern and Dr. Benezra referred us to a perinatal specialist for vigilante analysis and monitoring.

In addition, our son was in breech position, meaning that he had not made the positional change where the head is facing the birth canal. Instead, he was facing butt first which meant that he would have to be delivered by C-section.

Even with the most advanced diagnostics and expertise, the perinatologist could not figure out the cause for the growth restriction, and worse, our baby's heart was experiencing periodic decelerations, essentially periods where his heart rate would drop for no apparent reason. It was decided that Melissa would go in for constant fetal heart monitoring to make certain that the decelerations did not increase.

36 weeks into term, our tiny boy only 4 ½ pounds started displaying troubling decelerations. Dr. Benezra was not on service, but one of the other the OBGYN's on his team recommended immediate hospitalization for Melissa with round the clock monitoring of her vitals and that of the baby.

The next morning, thankfully Dr. Benezra was the on call OBGYN. He walked in and greeted us at 7 AM and asked Melissa, "Are you ready to have a baby?" He did not want to risk our son's life any further and was confident that while he would be born small, he was far enough along in his term that his team would be able to stabilize him.

Despite Dr. Benezra's confidence and knowing that he had one of the best OBGYN reputations in Central Florida, we were very nervous. At under 5 pounds, there was a very high chance that our son would have to be placed in the NICU to keep him stable and there was a neonatal specialist present in the OR prepared to take all necessary action in the event our baby was not stable.

C-sections generally proceed with the mother awake with a spinal injection of anesthesia administered to numb the surgical area. There was a curtain placed in front of her face so as not to see the surgeon and nurses working.

Dr. Benezra quickly discovered the reason for our son's lack of growth and the heart decelerations: his umbilical cord was wrapped around his neck three times. Dr. Benezra removed the baby and my wife and I heard his immediate cry and tears of joy flowed from both of us. Austin Lee Welton officially joined this world and blessed our lives the morning of June 19, 2008 by emergency C-section.

The neonatologist was a really cool guy and encouraged me to come over and see my baby and his evident lack of concern was a relief to me. Austin was grabbing the doctor's pinky with authority and the doctor told me, "Wow, great grip for a 4.6 pound child!" His breathing was fine and Austin was 100% stable. He would not have to go to the NICU as we had feared.

The neonatologist informed us that his stature would catch up in the next 6-8 months, especially because Melissa was committed to breastfeeding. His growth restriction would have no permanent effects and Austin would be fine.

In fact, not only did Austin catch up in less than 6 months, he would go on to remain consistently in the 95th percentile for height for the duration of his childhood. My wife's side of the family has a great deal of height among the males and Austin clearly inherited that. As of the writing of this book, Austin is 11 years old, 5'4", 109 pounds, and is a strong lacrosse player, able to shoot the ball 65 miles per hour.

Austin also has an incredibly active and imaginative mind, is an avid reader, and is curious about the world, especially in science. He is extremely athletic, able to master anything he tries. Beyond lacrosse, he is a surfer, skier, and certified diver.

I could not have hand picked a better son for me. I am a proud Dad!

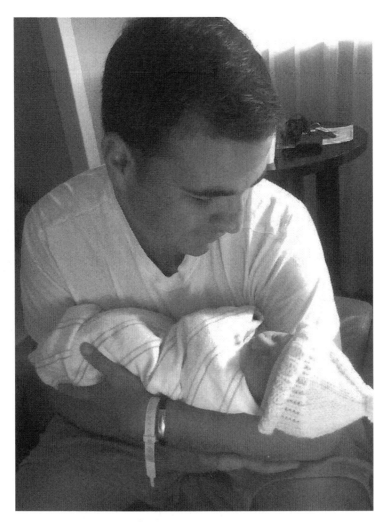

Austin Lee Welton with Dad June 19, 2008

Austin Lee Welton with Mom Summer 2009

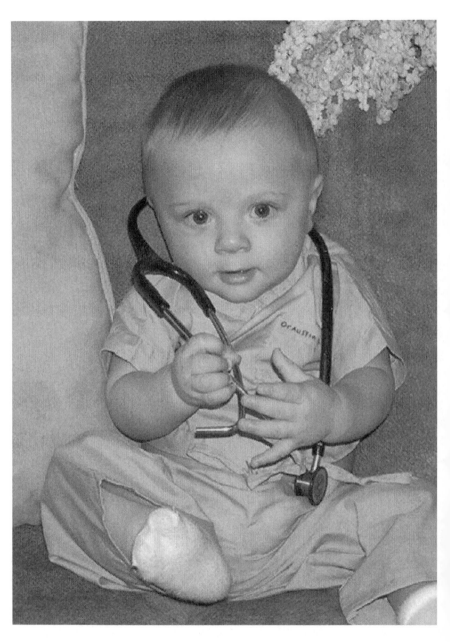

Austin Lee Welton dressed like Daddy Spring 2009

Austin Lee Welton Summer Faceoff Tournament June 2018

Chapter 33 - "Financial illiteracy is like being in a rain storm and trying to jump in between the raindrops... eventually it all catches you at the same time." – *Johnnie Dent Jr.*

The signs of the pending financial crisis were there long before President Bush came on the air in September of 2008, but I among many consciously chose not to heed the warnings. Every credible financial expert predicted it and home values were already starting to rapidly decline in Florida as early as late 2006, the state many would say was ground zero for the coming economic collapse.

Still, I continued business as usual enjoying phenomenal growth through my strongest year 2008 when the practice growth was just shy of having doubled the gross revenue of the practice when I had purchased it just 4 years earlier. My blinders were on so badly and I was so oblivious of what was to come, even after President Bush came on the air to inform the American people of the necessary bailout of the failed banking giants (later to be called TARP), with business still coming in strongly, I was still gearing up to advertise to hire a second veterinarian in 2009.

I have most of my existence been a consummate optimist which has mostly served me well but has on occasion also served as a curse when the optimism has led to an inability (or unwillingness) to see the downside of circumstances. The optimist trait empowered me to reach for heights of veterinary medical and surgical experience and expertise most general practitioners never aspire to, while empowering me to purchase a practice at the unusually young age of just barely 30.

With the birth of my son Austin and flying high on being a Dad, it was even extra hard for me to see the negative side of anything. As far as I was concerned, all was right in the world and no one was going to tell me otherwise.

Beyond blind optimism, however, I was also influenced to a major degree by my former employer, Dr. Hank Travis, who did not get caught up in analysis and detail but made business decisions based more on his gut and simple macro analysis like gross income and year to year growth. He never really dug down into the numbers, budgeted or benchmarked to assure that the business was in a healthy state. Record gross revenue does one no one any good if 90 cents of every dollar is still going out the door in expenditures.

To be fair to Hank, however, he did not really have to dig too much into the numbers. When I was working for his practice, veterinary medicine was still in its golden age that had started in about 1995 and extended until 2004. This gilded age of veterinary medicine was driven by two major new beneficial realities: pets had become beloved members of the families like no other time in history, and there was a new market of internal and external parasite preventive medications that took the pet world by storm.

Fleas, ticks, heartworm and other parasites were beyond a nuisance, they were serious health concerns. Fleas and ticks caused and spread disease and heartworm was common and deadly. Before the advent of safe and effective preventatives, these were rampant health concerns for pets.

Beyond being invaluable for the health of pets, the sale of preventative was also a great driving revenue source for veterinary practices. Thus, any deficiency in the running of the business and failing to analyze business data was easily made up for by this novel revenue stream.

In 2004 when I purchased my veterinary hospital, online pharmacies started competing in earnest with the brick and mortar pharmacies of veterinary clinics. This trend pushed forward despite the veterinary pharmaceutical companies pushing back against it, even filing class action lawsuits against companies like Pet Med Express and 1-800-Pet Meds.

The lawsuits were based on the fact that the veterinary pharmaceuticals intended for the preventatives to be sold solely through veterinarians so that the veterinarians would be responsible for the oversight of quality control and proper handling, storage, and product support once the products left their distribution centers. The way the online pharmacies were getting product was what is known as sideways sale, unscrupulous (mostly large animal veterinarians) purchasing products and diverting them at a small mark-up to online outlets.

This created major concerns that the quality, integrity, and safety of the products could be adversely affected in the process of changing so many hands. There were also reports of bogus product being counterfeited.

The pharmaceutical industry lost the lawsuits and online retailers became our new normal. The pharmaceuticals pushed back once again by refusing to guarantee the efficacy and safety of their products unless purchased anywhere other than a licensed veterinarian. They also started tracking the products and cracking down on product diverting veterinarians by cancelling their contracts but none of this seemed to slow down the growth of online veterinary preventive sales.

The consumers also remained un-phased when we educated them about quality control, lack of product guarantee, and risk of bogus or overseas products when purchased online. The industry even tried price matching the ridiculously low prices of online retailers and even that barely made a dent. We would later learn that we were wasting our efforts and our breath by trying to fight the growing trend of online pet medication sales, as 75% of people that purchased pet meds online did so not for cost savings, but more than anything, for convenience.

The point of all of this background is that a major source of veterinary practice revenue was contracting well before the Great Recession and we as an industry were trying to fight it rather than what we should have been doing, which was adapt to the new reality. The gilded age of veterinary medicine was over and we no longer had the cushion to protect us from lack of budgeting and being poor business people in general.

The truth is that most veterinarians are not good business people. We traditionally feel that if we do a good job, treat the patients and clients well, and conduct ourselves ethically, everything will be fine. There is some truth to that even today, but the reality is that there were forces at work in place well before the Great Recession that were changing the face of veterinary medicine that the Great Recession put a final and definitive stamp on.

Veterinary economic data could only accurately but trusted only as recently as 1974. In an issue of veterinary economics, the data showed that in every recession from 1974 up to the Great Recession, veterinary medicine still enjoyed an average of 4% growth. This suggested that the veterinary industry was solidly recession proof.

The Great Recession would prove that notion to be false. A March 2009 article from the Veterinary Information Network cited a study of 108 hospitals across the country that illustrated that 80% of hospitals reported zero to negative growth that year with 16% having to lay off personnel to continue to stay open.

After the post-holiday lull in early January, my wife and I found that historically, business typically gradually increased until fully hitting stride once again in March and maintaining a high pace until back to school time. In March of 2009, we clearly observed that the post-holiday lull had only marginally improved and as we watched the business account get smaller, we started to become increasingly concerned.

As the lull continued into the second quarter, we announced to our staff that to avoid staff layoffs that we would have to freeze raises and bonuses for the foreseeable future, as well as on a fair rotating basis, have staff go home early if we were not busy. For our part, Melissa and I had to date never taken a raise, investing our profits back into the practice that when we had purchased was in much need of facility and equipment upgrades. We would also have to learn to live on even less.

In the end, 2009 was downright frightening and dispiriting after all of the great progress we had made. All told in 2009 we went from healthy, steady growth to being down just over 10.1%. When you factor in that a business has to maintain growth of about 3.9% just to keep pace with the rate of inflation (the decrease in the value of the dollar that increases the cost of doing business and cost of living each year) just to break even, as devastating as a 10% loss sounds, it is even more devastating than even that.

My optimistic nature had never been so challenged in my professional life to date. With a very active brain with no shut off switch, insomnia had always been an issue for me. 2009 made it far worse. What kept me from true despair were three important aspects of my life: the sheer joy my baby boy brought me, knowing I was not alone in this struggle with my wife sharing the burden with me, and knowing that if in the end if things got worse and the unimaginable happened and I could not keep the clinic afloat, at least I was still a seasoned veterinarian that would still be able to have a job somewhere and support my family.

2010 was not really any better than 2009 but midway through the year we realized that while there was no growth, there was no further contraction in growth. We seemed to have reached the bottom of the abyss and we did not have to let anyone go. We hardly felt comfortable but we were toughing it out.

In 2009 despite the economic downslide, I had bitten the bullet and invested enrollment in an advanced reconstructive surgery of the canine knee course to gain certification and expertise on the latest reconstructive surgery techniques that had come out extensive research from University of Missouri and Texas A & M. While I had already been repairing knees for years with a still widely used technique, the certification brought clients of not just my county but from all over Florida seeking this kind of repair for their dogs giving our practice a special niche.

In early 2010, I had a career and practice changing experience at the North American Veterinary Conference when I was intrigued one morning to see a lecture titled "Veterinary Rehabilitation and Regenerative Medicine," being hosted by the Colorado State University department of surgery. The main theme of the lecture was the introduction of a new non-surgical regenerative therapy modality called low level class IV laser.

Not only were the clinical results and data irrefutable, when you have surgeons (whose primary goal is to cut and fix) coming out strongly in support of a non-surgical therapeutic approach, that is remarkable. However, in addition to being a useful non-surgical treatment option, in cases where surgery was unavoidable, it was also a great post-operative recovery tool that increased healing rates by 40%. There was also zero downside with no negative side effects and the patient felt little more than a slight vibration and some warmth of the laser head when the treatment was applied.

I ended up spending the whole day of lectures in that particular hall as the lecturers expanded from introduction to specific therapeutic applications of therapy laser in general practice. While the benefits of laser seemed virtually endless, the one benefit that really stuck out to me was its benefit for cases with spinal disc disease.

Dogs commonly injure their backs and the most common type of injury is herniated spinal disc. Disc herniation can cause anything from severe pain to partial and complete paralysis of the limbs. Up until the introduction of therapy laser, anti-inflammatories, steroids, muscles relaxers and rest were our only real solutions to disc herniation and when they failed, effective but very expensive decompression surgeries were the only option. Even in a good economy, such expensive surgeries were a tough sell to owners that had to weigh the love of their pet with the financial stability of their family. In an economy as dismal as the Great Recession, such a surgery had become virtually a non-existent option.

It dawned on me that in addition to my expanded reconstructive knee surgery niche, I could add the postoperative healing benefit of laser as well as offer a non-surgical alternative to spinal disc injuries that are so common in clinical practice that rarely a week goes by that we do not see one. I made the decision to hit the conference exhibit room floor to take advantage of a good deal on the therapy laser (veterinary conference exhibit hall vendors often offer special conference discounts for medical equipment). I settled on the Cutting Edge Laser. While the practice could hardly afford it, I saw the therapy laser as not only a great service to offer my clients and patients, but also as a means that would create another niche that would further differentiate and add value to my clinic.

Within a couple of months of receiving my laser in February of 2010, it was in constant use. At the time being the only clinic in the county that had a therapy laser, the word got out fast and I started getting second opinion cases seeking the alternative option for laser.

Word had gotten out so far and wide that the laser got the attention of a local magazine called Space Coast Medicine who wanted to do a piece on the laser and asked to interview me, as well as a few clients that would offer testimonials of which there was no shortage of. Following the interviews a photographer came in for a photo shoot and we ended up being the featured article in the next issue.

The article started bringing in clients from the furthest reaches of the county seeking laser therapy for their pets, some driving as far as 45 minutes to an hour away (Brevard County is 70 miles long). It was good for business, but beyond that, it was great high tech medicine that saved and prolonged countless lives.

When I had mentioned earlier that the laser was career changing, I was referring to not just laser, but to the introduction to a whole new paradigm of veterinary medicine. As I continued to attend additional rehabilitation lectures covering expanding applications of therapy laser, many of these symposiums were hosted by veterinarians that specialized in various forms of holistic or alternative veterinary medicine. As a results and data based veterinarian, up until this point in my career, I was generally quite limited in my consideration for alternative medicine because there was simply very little objective research to support its efficacy. Most of what was out there was based on anecdotal opinion and that just was not enough to convince me.

With the advent of therapy laser, however, a whole new field of veterinary medicine gradually emerged that became widespread enough that research grants were getting allocated to enable the opportunity for real scientific study to take place for management of disease through nutrition, nutritional supplements, acupuncture, chiropractic, and ultrasound pulse therapy among many others.

I still remained a primarily western trained and practicing veterinarian and relied on beginning my approach with good diagnostics and direct management of disease. However, by being open to and educated in alternative medicine, I now endeavored to prop up my patient's intrinsic healing mechanisms to help their bodies heal themselves.

Over time, I continued to pay special attention to research in this field and expanded my clinical practice to now include cannabis, PRP, and stem cell therapy. This subsequently will help us potentially wean off dependence on drugs faster, avoid surgery, or vastly improve surgical outcomes.

Returning to 2010, I felt this was a recovery year for us, not in the sense that there was a huge turn around in the financial stability of the practice, but we had managed to stop the bleed in part through expanding our niche services. I was finding joy in practice again because, by expanding treatment options for our patients, we saved and improved lives in ways that no other clinics in our area were doing, with the others still too stuck in the dogma of always mandating the western approach of treating the disease directly only.

The other amazing experience we enjoyed in 2010 was my wife becoming pregnant with our second child!

There is a bit of humor when it comes to our second child. When Melissa was pregnant with Austin, wanting to see him all the time and so curious about the baby's gender, we ultrasounded Melissa just about every time she was in the clinic. Prior to our official ultrasound appointment with an actual human ultrasonographer to learn the gender of our child, I was pretty confident that Austin was a boy having noted what was clearly to me, male genitalia. I turned out to be right.

With the second pregnancy we did the same thing and again and once again, I was confident that there were male genitalia. Melissa and I both liked the idea of having a girl for our second child, but we were ecstatic with whatever we got with healthy being our biggest wish. Near 100% certain this child would be our last, Melissa joked about preparing to live in a household of all males and to boot, we would not have to change the decor of the nursery.

Melissa had her official ultrasound appointment when we would learn the official gender of the baby while I was ironically away in Texas on an ultrasound conference. Convinced that I already knew the gender of the baby and previous ultrasounds having shown that the baby was healthy, I did not give it much thought and forgot about the visit. When I called home, Melissa did not remind of the visit or bring it up at all.

The reason for her silence was that she wanted to surprise me when I returned home that I was wrong this time and we were in fact having a girl, which she did the moment I walked through the door! I was already so far in boy mode with almost 2 year old Austin and having fully believed that the next was to be a boy; I had to process it for a moment and prepare to change gears.

I immediately thought about my Dad when my sister was born and how that had changed him (to date, he had been raising only my brother and I for the past 9 years). My brother and I watched with amusement as my kind but rather stoic Dad transformed into a mush with our little sister. To this day their bond is very special and just shy of 40 years old, my sister Leslie remains Daddy's Little Girl.

When Scarlett Isabella Welton was born on September 30, 2010, I had a full understanding of how my Dad felt about my sister. I felt like I was holding a precious little princess that I was sworn to love and protect with my life.

Scarlett followed in her brother's footsteps in becoming a strong lacrosse player, but her main passion is one she shares with my wife, which is showing Hunter-Jumper horses.

Scarlett Isabella Welton 2010

Scarlett Isabella Welton 2011

Scarlett Isabella Welton 2013

Scarlett Isabella Welton, Austin Lee Welton 2015

Scarlett Isabella Welton 2017

Scarlett's birth punctuated a year that marked a turnaround of my 2010 present and future. Although times were still not easy, I was full of hope and I was grateful beyond measure.

Chapter 34 - Hope is a good thing, maybe the best of things, and good things never die." – *Andy Dufresne (Shawshank Redemption)*

Perhaps there were enough prayers sent my way or the stars aligned just right for me during the 2010 North American Veterinary Conference. In addition to finding hope for a brighter day with my discovery of therapy laser and a window into alternative medicine, I also ran into Dr. Tony Warlick, a classmate of mine from Ross.

Tony was not among my closest friends but we were part of a general social group that liked to have fun when time allowed and we talked often. I would say we were friends in a unique sort of way in that we got along but there existed an unstated competitive rivalry between us. Still, I liked Tony and I respected his intelligence, competence and ambition.

Reconnecting was effortless, as we had both matured beyond the competitiveness of vet school and we were both genuinely happy for one another. He was a practice owner as well, happily married, with a daughter and two twin boys. Ultimately, it would be Tony who put me on to the CEO of the vendor who sold me my laser at that conference after getting a fancy steak dinner out of him (Tony had recently purchased a surgical laser from the same company). After the conference we intended to keep in touch and try to catch up at future conferences.

About a year later, Tony contacted me on Facebook to see if I would be interested in joining a veterinary study group for practice owners that would focus on best practices and strategies for individually owned clinics facing new modern challenges in the veterinary medical field. Internet pharmacies was ultimately just one of the modern challenges which also now included high volume/low cost spay, neuter, vaccine clinics that were already previously popping up, but had become popular during the recession.

These clinics charged a fraction of what a full service practice would charge, provided a third rate service for it, but were successful in selling it as equal to what high quality clinics do and devaluing these services in the eyes of many pet owners. It essentially was transforming well visits and sterilization surgeries into commodity services where, to a significant fraction of the pet owning population, made it acceptable to bargain shop these aspects of veterinary medicine and surgery.

There were even what we call "shot wagons," that were little more than a vet that showed up in a van at a gas station or in a pharmacy parking lot that would dole out vaccines from the back of the van. That is how low the profession had sunk in the midst of financial hardship.

Tony told me it would be minimal commitment, only some brief travel twice a year. Still slogging through the recession and cognizant of all of these aforementioned challenges, I agreed. He told me once the group was formed, a facilitator would reach out and highlight the next steps I needed to take.

I did not give it much more thought after Tony's outreach, but several months later I was contacted by a gentleman named Paul about my participation in an organization called Veterinary Study Groups. He explained to me the basic premise was that the organization put veterinary practice owners from all over the country in subgroups of 20 called a Veterinary Management Group to meet twice a year, compare financial data, and work together to help one another improve. The subgroup was part of larger organization of hundreds of practice owners that as a whole enjoyed special purchasing agreements with veterinary vendors and reference labs. Between benchmarking our financial data and getting purchasing agreements, VMG, as we all came to nickname the organization, in a nutshell was formed to help sustain the individually owned small practices by using collective numbers to even the playing field with the large corporate invasion that was yet another new challenge faced by the individually owned small practices.

My particular VMG is VMG 17. Our first meeting was held close to my home, only a 3 hour drive away in Amelia Island, FL. Despite Paul's brief overview of the basic tenants of VMG, I still was very unsure of what to expect. Outside of Tony, I did not have any idea who else was even in my group.

At the welcome dinner in a restaurant near our hotel, I met my group. I was surprised to see the diversity of members ranging from the youngest that was a few years younger than me (I was 38 at the time), to members that were well into their 40's and even mid to late 50's. There were smaller practices, larger practices, and a couple members owned multiple practices. After mingling for a bit we sat down and our facilitator spoke.

Our facilitator, Dr. Don Canfield was a member of the original VMG 1 that started the organization in 1984. Well into successful retirement, Don was no longer practicing but instead helping VMG to mentor groups. We were fortunate to be one of them.

I will never forget Don's first words as he spoke to us. After the formalities of thanking us for giving VMG a chance and participating, he counselled us to check our egos at the door, to forget what we thought we knew, be open to exciting new ideas, and to always remind ourselves who our worst enemy is by looking in the mirror.

In preparation for the meeting, we had to compile all of our financial data to present to the group. The data would be fed into a tracking system that compiled data for our group for comparison among one another, among VMG global, and among the top 20 most profitable hospitals. With such sensitive information, we all had to sign confidentiality agreements as we presented our "State of My Union" (SOMU) to be analyzed and critiqued by the group. Beyond numbers, our SOMU would also include all aspects of our practice including culture and human resources, even personal aspects of our lives.

In the process of presenting my own and participating in other SOMU presentations I learned that my story was not unique. Some were worse off than I was, some were better off. Most felt as I did that we had reached a point that we generally felt we were running in a hamster wheel with no destination or real vision in sight. The one thing we all had in common was the ambition to improve and be our best selves for our businesses, our employees and our families.

In addition to the SOMU presentations, the meetings also have content providers from every aspect of business, from leadership and HR, to accounting, marketing, and estate planning. Thus, 20 entrepreneurs benefit from one another's insight, as well as outside proven business experts. Don Canfield our facilitator alone was an incredible wealth of insight and inspiration. Few people in life had impressed me like Dr. Don Canfield.

I left my first VMG meeting humbled at how much business training I still needed all of these years into practice ownership and how much work I had to do to make up for lost time. I learned that yes, the recession and the new challenges of veterinary practice made things more difficult, but in the end, the real problem was a lack of any focus on attention to the business. I had always been proud of the medicine my practice put forth, but in the end, veterinary practices are businesses that need to be run as such. Had my business been in a better position in 2009, I could have weathered the recession with far less pain. Had I possessed a better ability to adapt to modern challenges rather than push back, things would have been easier.

But as it is commonly said, hindsight is always 20/20. I was indeed humbled but very excited for my future seeing so much opportunity ahead of me by just paying attention to financial data, running the practice more efficiently, and improving culture. My fellow VMG 17 members were similarly excited and rather than dwell on the mistakes of our past, we instead looked forward to a future of life abundance that righting our mistakes would provide.

A few months later, another opportunity came along that took me by surprise. Between the economy really rebounding by late 2012 and the practice doing better overall as the result of VMG initiatives I was implementing, after 4 years since I had been so close, I was finally once again seeing the near future necessity to add a second veterinarian.

Literally the week I was thinking about this, I got a note on my desk stating that Dr. David Fogelberg was inquiring about possible employment at my practice. I had met Dave several times before, including at my alma mater's North American Veterinary Conference alumni reception. Dave and I were both

Ross graduates but missed one another by 2 years (he had left island and gone on the start his clinical year at University of Minnesota in 1996, I arrived in 1998).

Dave had just left one of my biggest competitors, a large practice located on the beachside following a 16 year tenure. Between what I had heard about Dave and his stellar reputation as a veterinarian in our area and what I knew of him always being a personable gentleman when we ran into one another socially, I was immediately interested in pursuing this.

Of course, mine was not the only practice interested in courting Dr. Fogelberg and others were in the running. After a 16 year tenure with another practice, Dave was going to be patient with his decision and we agreed that he start a part time employment arrangement with us and engaged in several lunch meetings to discuss what our ideal employment arrangement would look like.

Over time, not only was I convinced that he was exactly the right fit for the vision I had for taking my practice to the next level, we became good friends in the process. Dave apparently shared the same feelings and officially joined the practice as a full time associate in January, 2013. Not only had I finally been able to expand with a second veterinarian, but I was fortunate to do so with the best free agent on the market so to speak.

Also in 2013, my Mom at 67 years old had moved on to official, well deserved retirement. She and my Dad had left the imprints of their love all over the practice, the greatest of which was the "west wing" that my parents had donated the money for. When I bought the practice, as I alluded to in an earlier chapter, most of the west side of the hospital was a screened in porch and it was wasted space, only able to house a refrigerator, the freezer to hold bodies awaiting cremation, and some storage boxes.

During that dismal year of 2009, my Dad found a contractor that enclosed the porch replacing the screened areas with glass block, added air conditioning and heating, and had the floor finished. The main screened in region of the old porch became a break room for the staff, but the enclosing of the porch in also enabled us to renovate and nearly double the size of our adjacent operating room and build a new manager's office.

My parents have supported me with all their hearts all of my life. Their contributions to and participation in the clinic was a natural extension of that. This addition and renovation to this day is a physical reminder of their unconditional love every day I walk into work and they gifted it to us at a time when the practice was facing its most difficult challenges.

With Mom retiring, I was in need of a practice manager. I was hardly a human resources expert, but it was general common knowledge that when seeking a new manager, it is best to hire from outside the practice, as an employee promoted into a position of leadership in a small business often runs into resistance of employees now finding themselves having to take directives from a formerly equal colleague.

Dave had a close friend, Ingrid Culver, who had worked with him at his previous practice for 12 years as a veterinary technician and was currently working in the most reputable veterinary specialty referral center in our county. I knew of her because on Dave's suggestion during his part time tenure, my mom had previously invited her to lunch to show us some ways that we could utilize our practice management software to implement some of the changes we were trying to make, the chief of which was to transition the practice to going paperless.

Dave made the introduction and several meetings later, we had a new practice manager. During the course of our meetings, I learned clearly that she was just what I was looking for. With a practice very much in transition and heading into unchartered territory, I needed a person with large body of experience in the industry, but one that was new to management, that would not come in with preconceived notions; to gradually grow into her position and remain malleable and adaptive, remain flexible in adopting policy and processes that met the challenges that were unique to our clinic. Ingrid also possessed a sense of humility where she would not hesitate to seek the council of colleagues she had nurtured friendships with throughout her tenure working in the veterinary field.

My Mom has spoken to me of seasons in our lives. Seasons could be periods of friendships that do not necessarily end badly, but run their course as we gain new friendships in the next stages of our lives. Seasons could be career and business transformations and awakenings of sorts that change our paradigms, our outlooks, and how we conduct our careers.

The season of figuring things out through trial and error and making decisions on gut instinct was past. I saw what had worked and what did not work but still had a long way to go. My journey of my new season had begun with joining VMG and progressed into truly running Maybeck Animal Hospital as a corporation with a leadership team, pyramid of leadership, documented processes that all the team were accountable to, with budgeting and benchmarking.

With the growth that came organically from the nation coming out of the recession and the addition of Dave, the clinic was able to afford consultants to come in and help us establish and maintain culture, maximize efficiency, and keep the financial benchmarks in the right percentages. Our leadership team engages in ongoing leadership training as a group and individually and as of the writing of this book, Ingrid is only a few months away from sitting for her exam to earn her practice management certification.

Our leadership team consists of Dave, Ingrid and I as permanent members. The other two members are voted in by the staff on a yearly basis to represent them on the leadership team; one from the front desk staff, one from the veterinary technician team. We meet once every two weeks at 7:30 AM over breakfast off site to iron out concerns, issues and wrinkles in practice logistics and report our collective conclusions that Ingrid presents at our monthly full staff meetings for greater discussion.

Through the efforts led by Ingrid with the whole medical team behind her, we achieved what I had previously thought impossible given the constraints of our facility; we achieved accreditation by the American Animal Hospital Association (AAHA) that I had mentioned in an earlier chapter. AAHA is an organization the supports best practices and conducting a veterinary practice by a veterinary university standard. It is a voluntary accreditation that requires a rigorous audit process both initially and then once every two years to verify that the practice continues to meet the AAHA standard.

In this way we tell the world that we practice medicine and run a veterinary clinic by the highest standard. Logistically, it holds us all accountable to best practices and reminds us to never give in to the temptation to cut corners. AAHA accredited hospitals also attract the best employee talent in the industry that naturally gravitate toward clinics that operate at the highest standard. Recall that in my search for my first position as a veterinarian, AAHA accreditation was very important.

This past October, 2018, we added a third veterinarian, Dr. Amanda Johnston. Amanda was a University of Florida graduate with a bachelor's degree in Animal Sciences. She applied for employment at Maybeck Animal Hospital in 2012 with the intention of making a career change to gain experience while she completed some remaining prerequisite courses to apply for veterinary school and ended up working for us for three years before getting accepted to none other than Ross University.

Amanda was a reliable and enjoyable person to work with during her years as a technician working for us. When she came back during her clinical year to work externships with us with me as her primary mentor, it seemed as if she had never left, only she now possessed the skills of a doctor. Having been raised in our culture, she was right fit for our first new graduate hire.

I am very excited that both Dave and Ingrid will be becoming full partners in Maybeck Animal Hospital this year. We are also currently in negotiations as partners to purchase a second veterinary practice that is for sale to the south of us.

The most important lessons I have learned as a leader is to speak less and listen more, mandate less and rather seek answers through consensus. I am more keenly aware of my strengths and my weaknesses and understand that my optimist nature is an asset but can also be a hindrance. I have more faith than ever that in gaining consensus from the talented people I have been fortunate to surround myself with; we will arrive at the best possible conclusions.

Chapter 35 - "Some beautiful paths cannot be discovered without getting lost." – *Erol Ozan*

At so many turns along my journey, there existed the real possibility that I would not ultimately fulfill my life's goal to become a doctor of veterinary medicine. In hindsight, as I see the different permutations and combinations that could have led to different outcomes, the fact that I am here writing this book as a doctor of veterinary medicine would seem among the least probable of outcomes.

I have zero doubt, however, that becoming a veterinarian was my true path. My childhood best friend, Steve Jordan (now an impressive and successful celebrity trainer in Los Angeles) has often commented about the change he saw in me from childhood through the present. He observed the younger version of me as kind of a slacker, coasting through life care free with little sense of urgency outside of lacrosse and girls. As I got locked in and earnestly pursued an education and career in veterinary medicine, Steve notice over time my transition from an attitude of indifference to relentless ambition to be the best possible version of myself I could be.

It has been amazing to get the perspective of a buddy (more like a bother) who knows me better than most people in this world, because the transition occurred so gradually and I was so preoccupied with my mission that I really did not give it much thought. He opened my eyes to the fact that it is not typical of the average veterinarian to venture into so many aspects of medicine, surgery, and alternative care. It is certainly not typical of a veterinarian to launch a media platform and business.

The journey and achievement of becoming a veterinarian awakened something in me that was lying dormant. Once I was on my true path, I seemed never to tire, always working and always being on the lookout for the next opportunity and that is still my reality today.

In my spare time when I am not working in my clinic, I am writing, podcasting, tweaking my websites, running a youth lacrosse club, coaching lacrosse, playing men's lacrosse, diving, boating, surfing, and working out. A friend recently asked me if there will ever come time that I sit still. I answered him, "How much fun would that be?"

In the process of reading this book, you may have noticed that my journey was hardly a cake walk. I made my journey harder from the outset through sheer lack of focus and urgency. I suffered loss in relationships, pets and people, and came across teachers that were more interested in exerting their power over students than mentoring them. I had an undergraduate advisor that tried to discourage me from attending the school that ultimately provided the means to my doctor of veterinary medicine degree.

Upon reflection, however, I have zero regrets. This was the way it had to be. This path was never meant to be easy for me. That would have been too boring!

Every challenge, every person and every event that created adversity in my journey remains as much a part of the veterinarian, father, husband, friend, and coach that I am today as the wonderful people like my parents and my great mentors that paved the way for me to believe in myself set the highest goals. We are the sum total of all of our collective experiences in life's journey and hard times are equally as important as the joyous ones.

Whether one is a person who wishes to pursue a career in veterinary medicine or not, I hope that all can take away some value in my story and know that:

- It is never too late to pursue your dreams.
- When you make mistakes, recognize them, endeavor not to repeat them, but forgive yourself and move on.
- Whatever you choose to do in life, pursue your goals guided first and foremost with love and you will do it exceptionally.

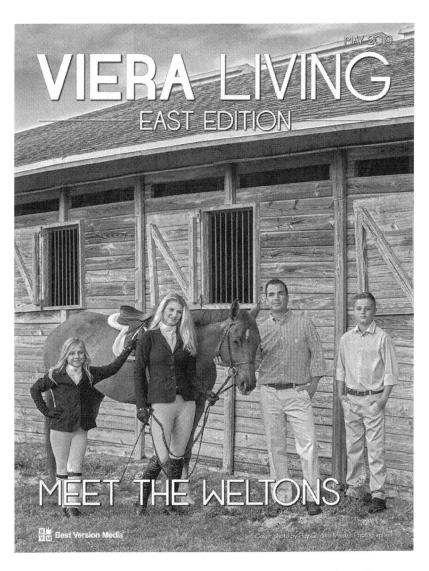

Roger and Family Named the April 2019 Featured Family in their Community Magazine

Made in the
USA
Columbia, SC